TAKT-ICAL LEADERSHIP

LEADERSHIP

Lean Management Techniques
to Achieve Sustainable Improvement

by LOWELL J. PULS

AuthorHouse™
1663 Liberty Drive
Bloomington, IN 47403
www.authorhouse.com
Phone: 1 (800) 839-8640

Published by AuthorHouse 03/13/2019

ISBN: 978-1-5462-7044-7 (sc)
ISBN: 978-1-5462-7194-9 (hc)
ISBN: 978-1-5462-7045-4 (e)

Library of Congress Control Number: 2018914102

Print information available on the last page.

Any people depicted in stock imagery provided by Getty Images are models,
and such images are being used for illustrative purposes only.
Certain stock imagery © Getty Images.

This book is printed on acid-free paper.

Because of the dynamic nature of the Internet, any web addresses or links contained in this book may have changed
since publication and may no longer be valid. The views expressed in this work are solely those of the author and do
not necessarily reflect the views of the publisher, and the publisher hereby disclaims any responsibility for them.

authorHOUSE®

Introduction

"The truest definition of waste is working to become more efficient at something you shouldn't be doing in the first place."

Running a business is complicated work, from the basic concepts of strategizing, planning, execution, and adjustment; to accounting, engineering, customer service, and human resources. These individual business functions can assume a mission, goals, and an agenda all of their own, often individually disconnecting in some way from the essential business mission of being the very best at servicing the needs of a target market. Applying this book's concepts in a basic step-by-step fashion will enable you to find your own approach, adapting to each business condition. In any successful enterprise, the process solutions can be flexible but once established, the process disciplines can't be compromised. Leveraging the simplicity of the lean approach to "standard work," these chapters are written in a "major step" (the key concept being communicated), "key points" (what is required to assure a perfect, quality result), and the "reason why" (because communicating or explaining the intent behind an action is critical to selling an acceptance of the disciplines). If this book doesn't help simplify your approach to aligning activities and improving performance in your own business, I encourage you call me for a translation.

Forty-three years in manufacturing and business have led me to believe that although I haven't *seen* everything, I'm fairly sure I've *stood next to it* at one time or another. My experiences have amassed many stories that are fun to tell, and the story parts of this book are woven from a collection of true incidents to provide supporting examples. A few of those who experienced them with me might even recognize the situations.

If there is one overarching theme in this book, it is *Takt*. *Takt* is a German word for the orchestra leader's baton that sets the rhythm of the performance. in Lean Enterprise/Lean Manufacturing, Takt represents the pace of market demand. Takt is translated into a time basis to provide the amount of time available to fulfill one unit of market demand. It is most important to understand that very few organizations actually do that math (calculating takt time), and most that do, calculate it only for their fulfillment processes, excluding their management (or business) processes. This is a critical error that ultimately could undermine the performance of the entire organization, and it can only be resolved by establishing an applicable time basis for every functional part of the organization. As you read, keep in mind the importance of takt. You will see how it can be truly transformational.

A close friend of mine likes to say that leaders are smart, complex people who don't believe simplification is possible. In truth, most of my experience suggests it isn't so much that they don't believe simplification is possible as it is that they aren't very good at simplifying something when they are in the middle of working on it – more focused on the mission than the process. The difficulty seems to come from their approach to responding to and solving problems in their business. Some leaders attempt to monitor and control excessive levels of detail, leaving them overtasked and impeding assistance from more appropriate subordinates who should own the task. They can develop "solution lock": that tendency to gravitate to a single solution for a problem earlier than the facts would suggest is appropriate. Even worse, leaders might cling to that solution even when it begins to prove sub-optimum.

One of my favorite examples of simplification comes from an old training room joke many have heard: A semi-truck gets wedged under an overpass. While the police, fire, and civil personnel are at a stalemate as to how get the truck out, a ten-year-old boy walks up and asks, "Why don't you just let the air out of the tires?"

There is yet another story that similarly illustrates this point. A great bow hunter heard of a teenager with a reputation as the greatest archer in the state—someone who never misses the bullseye. So, the famous hunter went to visit this boy and asked to see his practice range. The boy took him into his family's back yard, encircled by a wooden fence with more than a dozen targets on it. Directly in the center of each target was an arrow. The man was amazed. "You always get the arrow right in the center of the bullseye?" he asked. The boy nodded in assurance. When asked to demonstrate his skill, the boy fetched his bow and nocked an arrow. Drawing back the bow, he quickly sent the arrow into the wooden fence. Dropping the bow to the ground, he ran over to a bucket of paint sitting near the fence. In two quick arcs, he painted a ring around the arrow. Finished, he turns to the man and announced, "It works every time."

The objective of this book is to identify management behaviors and organizational circumstances that unnecessarily complicate initiatives, and provide simple solutions to nullify them. Once eliminated, the initiatives implementation itself is simplified, freeing up improvements in performance along the way and making them more sustainable. The essential message is that: Simplification is necessary in every situation and finding a simplified process will make your solutions more effective, readily transferable, and sustainable. There are a few concepts where I've intentionally minimized my explanations to frame a simplified the approach without prescriptive detail, leaving you the latitude of filling in the specifics of your own business's needs.

Also, because so many books have been dedicated to the topic of Lean, my purpose here is not to add to the count, but only to delve as deeply into Lean as is necessary to simplify the way you can apply it to manage your change initiative and clarify the impact it can have on sustainment

More than anything, after working to transform a variety of companies, I felt compelled to make a statement about how to sustain improvement, because, for so many reasons, it just doesn't happen. First, you must connect clear targets for improvement to the business mission—not to the careers of those in leadership roles. Second, if your leadership style isn't respectful of the human element—mainly in its power to propel your cause— you will very likely miss your goals. Finally, a leader must take great care to ensure that the objectives for the change initiative are "rooted" and that the benefits and successes can be shared by everyone involved. Integrity in management is foundational to sustainment, and high turnover at the leadership level will always undermine continuity. AJ Sheppard once wrote;

"Leading change means bringing people with you to a better state than any of you could have envisaged alone."

I hope you enjoy this semi-fictional chronical of my career experiences in manufacturing!

Lowell Puls

Acknowledgements

It takes a lot of help to write successfully, and I would like to express my gratitude to those who have helped along the way.

Cris Freese – Editor par excellence. Cris did an excellent job of editing the final manuscript and gave me valuable input to make it a better read.

Terry "Doc" Smith – Illustrator. Terry has provided me illustrations of his proprietary characters for several years now, and is always able to come up with something that communicates my message in a lighter, gently humorous way. Most of the illustrations in this book are by Terry.

Kathleen Fosbinder Smith – Graphic Artist – This is my first collaboration with Kathy, yet she was able to come up with the perfect cover design with minimal input on my behalf.

Wendy Puls – is the Graphic Artist who designed the RAD dude and Vinnie for my first book Keep It Simple and Sustainable. I have gladly re-used them in Takt-ical Leadership.

There are many more leaders who have contributed to these stories over the years and influenced my own way of thinking. I'd like to thank all of those I've worked with over the years for their own individual examples of leadership.

Family: All of them - Always!

Lowell Puls

Contents

Chapter 1: Leading with Vision

Walking the fine line between vision and hallucination to build a winning strategy.

1.1 Situation Analysis

1.2 Defining Your Vision

1.3 Communicating Your Vision

"Good morning Mr. Puls!" The front desk attendant interrupted her data input work instantly when I gave her my name. "I know the leadership team is anxiously awaiting your arrival. Please, you don't need to sign the guest register, after all, you *are* our new president."

She immediately picked up the desk phone and punched in an extension number. "Hello Maria, Mr. Puls is here. Should I show him to the conference room?" there was a short pause as she listened to the answer. "Very well, thank you."

"This way please." She led me down a long hall, adorned with framed photos of long-term employees, customer appreciation awards, and community recognitions. I looked at them with interest as we went by, on our way to a vacant conference room.

"Can I get you some coffee?" She asked pleasantly.

"Please do, and if you have it in IV form, just go ahead and plug me in." She chuckled at my comment.

Unfortunately for the current team, all of this customer goodwill was in the past, the newest award going on four years old. The business had been on a downhill slide for some time and at this point was truly at risk to lose come major accounts.

It would be my third turnaround from the leadership chair, having spent much of my prior career resolving business-critical issues such as scaling capacity to meet increasing market demand, cleaning up quality spills, replacing problem suppliers, and developing and implementing complex worldwide footprint strategies. Managing and deploying an appropriately paced sense of urgency comes easily to me, but based on what I'd learned during and after the interview process, this transformation would be a real test.

DFC-P Products Inc., with over $400M in revenue was besieged with both customer complaints and labor challenges, and was losing accounts quickly as a consequence of poor customer service. Somewhere along the way, they had lost their commitment to fulfilling their mission of delivering high quality products to their customers' expectations. Clearly disconnected from their market, they would need some serious "Lean Thinking" applied to their processes in order to get things moving forward again. Currently, their perspective was turned inward, tracking metrics that were more effective at rationalizing their poor performance rather than at meeting the expectations being demanded by the customers. Even their strategies regarding production and sales seemed to be in denial of the market itself.

I was doing this introduction alone, with the hiring manager based in Europe and unable to make it here in time. As I looked at some of their policy documents and metrics hanging on the wall, the management team members began to drift in to meet me.

"Hello, I'm Maria Adams, your Director of Human Resources.

"And I'm Geoff Little, head of Operations. With me is Dick Schuster, our game show host, I mean Vice President of Sales."

Dick gave him a light shove in shoulder for gigging him that way. "If I'm in charge of the game, at least it isn't a stoplight fire drill like the one in operations." Geoff was mute to that return shot.

"I'm Janet Kim, director of Supply Chain and Materials.

"Very pleased to meet you Janet, I've heard a lot of good things about you."

"I'm better late than never, John Riley, VP of Engineering!"

"And I'm just pleased to have you here." I responded warmly.

After a little bit of small talk, everyone took their seats so that we could begin.

"Well, I'm excited to be taking the lead on this performance transformation. The business has frankly been struggling, and some might refer to my involvement as a "last chance opportunity" to get it resurrected. In that vein, it's my intention to raise everyone's sense of urgency, but then to mute them as well. In other words, we all need to understand the realities of our situation, but then we mustn't panic, because it will make us less effective.

"My challenge for the coming weeks is to help you achieve an immediate impact on our quality and customer service levels. At the same time, we'll do a budget assessment to see how far off we really are. I'm looking forward to getting to know all of you, and plan to meet privately with each of you over the next few days to hear your views on the causes of these severe performance problems. Once we have all talked individually, I'll digest what I've heard, rephrase the details to preserve confidentiality, and feed a summary back to you as a team. We should then be better equipped to determine our best course of corrective action. It's critically important that you are open and honest about the problems, or else we'll waste time pursuing the wrong solutions. Until then, are there any questions?"

"Do you anticipate making any immediate changes?" asked Maria.

"Yes, to some of our processes – mostly to get containment around the key customer issues. Nothing with people at this time though. It's essential for the entire organization to develop confidence in this team and in me, because we'll really need everyone's trust going forward.

What that means is, we can't afford to flail around and make mistakes out of haste. I think a quote by John D. Rockefeller says it best;

"'Next to doing the right thing, the most important thing is to let people know you are doing the right thing.'

"I will want us to focus very hard on both the plan and the message. Once the interview process is complete, we'll all agree to a plan which can be executed with the appropriate urgency. That said, however, some changes are inevitable. Are there other questions?"

There was a nervousness about the room, and since there were no takers for my second offer, we put together a schedule for the individual interviews before adjourning.

Organizations that get into trouble usually do so for myriad reasons, but the results are typically anything but varied—they're simply bad. Like others I'd seen, this business was clearly in a "death spiral," that place where performance had deteriorated to a point where everyone was so immersed in problem resolution that essential business needs were being neglected, driving further deterioration in performance.

I knew there would be some suspicion and anxiety regarding my private interviews. Ronald Reagan once said the most feared words any organization could hear were, "I'm from the government, and I'm here to help you." Well, announcing, "I'm an outsider, and I'm coming in to turn your company around," must run a close second. To reduce those fears, I conducted the interviews, listened carefully, learned something personal about each of the management team, and asked the same series of scripted questions of each of them. At the end, I thanked each person for their candor and reiterated my commitment to make the ensuing report as generic as possible. As might be expected, some were cautious and tight-lipped, while others were bitter and quick to lash out over grievances, real or imagined. Still others were transparent, genuine, insightful, and honest.

A week later, we met for our first staff meeting to review the interview results. It seemed as if the team was a bit nervous, unsure of how their input would be used or how candidly my summary of their input might be. They were in for a surprise.

"Welcome, everyone." I opened positively, smiling to try and put them at ease. "Hopefully the past few days have been productive for you. It would seem that the temporary measures we have taken to contain some of our delivery issues are beginning to have a positive effect.

"I would really like you to understand how simple my approach will be. First, please try to erase any thoughts that everything around you is completely broken. This is an important message to spread to your teams, as well, because as we dig in to make permanent changes, we'll need everyone to believe in what they will be doing individually. Without this, our associates might view their efforts as hopeless, and they'll quickly return to 'muscling' processes for shreds of improvement, just maintaining the minimal performance they're already giving and guaranteeing defeat. Warren Buffet once said, *'The most important thing to do if you find yourself in a hole is to stop digging!'* We will need to be aware of our 'holes.' This organization, like every one, has things that are well done, and we'll have to identify and preserve them for two important reasons: first, we can save time by not trying to fix things that don't need to be fixed; and second, it's important we don't demotivate people by creating the impression that everything done here is badly done. People take pride in their work and preserving that which they do well is a great way to give them the credit they deserve. It will also allow us to better focus our improvement resources and efforts on the things that needs to be fixed. Once that is accomplished, we can establish an agenda to attack the initial target areas."

During the interview process, the team was unanimous in indicating that the company wasn't servicing their customers adequately nor fulfilling the commitments *we* were making to them. Our market research also confirmed the fact that we weren't delivering what they wanted or expected. As I engaged the team in a standard *"Five Why"* approach to our market issues, the input that the various team members had confidentially given me was selectively interjected. Not only did this keep the conversation stimulated, but it helped us narrow the list of root causes so that we could proceed toward addressing the primary issues.

"Why are customer service levels so poor?" I asked.

"Because their demand is so erratic that we can't forecast it properly," Geoff, the operations director, said.

"Well, yeah, but even if we forecast it correctly," injected Janet, our Director of Materials, "our manufacturing time is longer than the market lead time allows anyway."

I asked, "What *is* the market lead time?"

"Usually about sixteen weeks," said Dick, VP of Sales.

"Says who? How do we know?"

Dick looked somewhat confused. "Uh, because that's the lead time our competitors quote. It's kind of always been that way."

"Really? Okay, back up a minute." I paused. "Do we *always* quote 16 weeks?"

"Yes, we do," Dick stated flatly, as though this was common knowledge. "Well, most of the time we do. Sometimes we'll take an expedite order and push it through."

"I'm aware that a number of our products are custom built. Can anyone tell me what percentage?"

Dick shrugged. "One hundred percent. Shoot, everything we do is custom."

I looked over at John, our VP of Engineering. "Does that mean your people touch *every* order? Geesh, what's <u>your</u> typical process time?"

"Some things can be done in a week, but others can take up to a month. It all depends on the product, the customer request, and the level of engineering required."

I weighed that for a moment. "If every order is custom to some degree, then are they just custom-assembled, or do they require specially designed parts as well?"

"Special parts are often required and usually have two-to-four weeks of procurement time. We have some pretty responsive local suppliers," Janet answered.

I turned to her. "What are the longest lead-time parts we buy for our products?"

"It's the Asian stuff, so count on six months for steel foundry castings and around eighteen months on proprietary subassemblies."

I tapped a few notes to myself on my tablet. "Okay, Geoff, can you give me some kind of idea what your manufacturing time is like?"

"What, for normal runs? Sure. Usually, we can complete Product A in four weeks if it has minimal customization. Product C is always customized and can take up to twenty-six weeks to make and ship."

I sat quietly for a moment, writing more notes and organizing my thoughts. Finally, I looked up at the whole team. "So, if we take one to four weeks to engineer an order, then two weeks to eighteen months to buy the stuff that goes in our products without using a forecast, and finally four to twenty-six weeks to produce it, how on earth do we deliver anything in the sixteen weeks quoted?"

"We don't," Dick answered, somewhat sheepishly. "Leastwise, not very often."

"*How often*?" I asked him pointedly.

He swallowed. "Well…uh…other than the standard versions of product A, I can't remember the last time we did so."

I looked from one face to the next around the table. "Are you serious? Then why on earth do we quote it that way?"

"Have to," his tone was getting defensive. "If we didn't, we wouldn't get the order!"

I just stared at him, clearly taken aback. "What do our distribution partners think about us then?"

"Honestly, they think we're pretty incompetent. The only thing that keeps them coming back to us is the reputation of the equipment we build," Dick added.

"Okay, let's go back to *why*. Why are our customer service levels so poor? How did this happen?"

"Our systems are broken!" Maria from Human Resources said, jumping into the fray. Her flushed cheeks matched her curly red hair. She had been reticent to talk to me at first during our private appointment, but once I'd gained her confidence, she became a bit more comfortable, rattling off a checklist of things that had been bothering her for a long time. She wasn't trying to be a troublemaker. She had given fourteen years to the company and was fiercely loyal to it. Seeing it flounder was upsetting to her personally and professionally.

"Thanks for that blunt honesty, Maria. I think your confession of reality just opened a door that may lead to some potential answers for us. Okay, I want the same from the rest of you. We're behind closed doors, and no one is recording us, so go ahead and put the elephant on the table."

Walking through the remaining "whys" took a couple of hours, and I could see the frustration and concern building in each of them. However, at the same time, we were successfully narrowing down to our top priority: to restore our former high-quality customer service. Ultimately, it became obvious to everyone in that room that if our company couldn't make good on its commitments to delivery schedules, production excellence, and follow-up service, nothing else mattered. Forget the fancy advertising slogans, lucrative contracts, crisp uniforms, shiny delivery trucks, and service to the community. Without satisfied customers, none of the other stuff made a bit of difference. On that, we agreed, and having formed that consensus, I gave them a two-hour break to grab some lunch and to check in at their offices. At the same time, they were asked to mull over what we'd covered that morning and to come back in the afternoon with additional comments, suggestions, or even rebuttals.

* * *

When we re-convened, they seemed much more at ease and focused. Several of them had returned with tablet devices for notetaking. I was anticipating some lively interchanges and was not disappointed.

"Okay, now let's try to define the top three or four reasons why we're not meeting the needs of our clientele," I said.

"We can't forecast the business." Jolene, the financial director, blurted out. She had been somewhat subdued during the morning session, but I now saw that having some time to mentally process the discussion approach, she was ready to make her voice heard.

"Why?" I prodded. "And I'm speaking to the team, not just asking Jolene."

"Because Sales never commits to anything until it's a signed order—then it suddenly becomes a five-alarm fire," Geoff half mumbled, not disguising his disdain.

Dick winced at that. "Look, my team isn't made up of mind readers," he retorted sharply. "Our distributors can't tell when their customer is going to place an order, much less how large it's going to be, and they won't commit to placing a unit in their own inventory. We're the ones who keep the cash flow coming into this place. It's your job to see that orders get filled."

I raised my hands for peace. "All right, all right, let's look at that in a minute, folks. At the present time, how do you plan and purchase those long lead time materials that are six to eighteen months out?"

Janet intervened. "There's no immediacy to anything. We look at what the trends have been for the past two or three years, and hope that we'll be similarly fortunate for this year. So, we place orders based on history, because we clearly can't base them on actual orders-in-hand. The results are chaos. We're either way too short on one product, or we have a two-year stockpile of components for another. It's like rolling dice and it drives my team crazy."

Geoff gave a sarcastic chuckle. "Drives *you* crazy? Man, on the factory floor it's feast or famine. We either have big orders and no materials, or else we have warehouses full of materials that no one wants. My people will go from working double shifts and running up the overtime, to being sent home for nothing to do."

"So, what efforts have you made to try to level your production so that the factory and the materials teams can work on a level basis?" My prodding was working.

"We build Products A, B and D to inventory in the fall and winter," Janet and Dick said almost simultaneously.

"How can you do that if nearly everything is custom?"

They could sense my confusion.

"We build base units and then rework them, as needed, to make them order-specific," Geoff said.

"How do you cover the extra cost?"

"We don't! And sometimes the rework is extensive, really hurting our margins." John said.

"Okay, is it safe to say that much of this could be eliminated if you put some effort into your Sales and Operations Planning Process to stabilize your planning processes? It's often called S&OP for short."

They looked at me quizzically.

"We don't currently have a process by that name," Janet stated.

"It would seem you do." I answered back. "Only in this case, it sounds like it's called *Sold! —and Operations Panics!"* Geoff chuckled at that.

"It's my belief that every organization has information it can use to build a forecasting model. Right now, you're using backward information—history—to predict the future. The problem with that is that the future will never change if the past is used to drive it. Dick, what has been the historical sales for product B over the past five years?

"Relatively flat at about 25-30 units per year," he responded.

"And can you recall if we were forced to turn any orders away during that time?" I pressed on.

"Every year. Sometimes we lost the order to a competitor; sometimes the season ended before we filled the order, so they cancelled it."

"Then we're going to have to mine some additional data from all of the key directions: the distribution channel, economic data, our sales team, and anywhere else we can find a data point we think is relevant. After that we'll *place some bets!"*

As we proceeded, the list quickly expanded beyond the number one problem of forecasting. Soon they were also listing execution and engineering-derived product launch issues. Additionally, we uncovered a number of more minor procedural items, such as multi-tiered approval timing and system functionality issues, but we were able to agree quickly on ways to eliminate them, neutralize their impact, or cast them aside in order to focus on the larger problems. By this point we had successfully outlined our top organizational mission as "delivering to our customers in *their* required timeframe," which blossomed into three initial projects: 1) contain the operational issues that were impacting our delivery commitments, 2) compress our lead times, and 3) find a performance path back to budget.

Using a technique, I refer to as the Three C's (**C**ontain the problem, **C**orrect the problem, **C**ontinuously Improve beyond the problem), we started to address the containment of our performance challenges by sorting through the steps required to fulfill a customer order for each product and assign an immediate containment action, regardless of how it impacted us internally. The team worked diligently, but it took some time and effort to identify containment needs for the thorniest problems, as well as considerable patience in getting the team to drill down toward the root cause. As the team improved at building a complete, focused action plan for each issue (addressing what we knew and then highlighting what we needed to know more of), we held them all fast until everyone was ready to move to the next problem. In some cases, we chose to define the objective before deferring the containment exercise to a broader or smarter team. As they became used to the process, we began to pick up momentum. The group was just beginning to visualize a path toward resolving our issues for the customer.

Our efforts to address the next customer facing project—compressing our lead times—was even more challenging. Separating our supply chain lead times, our internal thruput time, and our forecasting opportunities under separate teams, it didn't take long for us to find improvement opportunities. Many of them were easily implemented and had a rapid effect.

Our third organizational imperative of finding a path back to achieving budget performance was a leap of faith from our current state. Here the discussion proceeded more quickly since most of the causes of budget noncompliance were driven by corrective or containment actions resulting from our customer satisfaction problems. We were able to identify project priorities readily, and we quickly established a path to generate improvement.

Once we had completed the containment lists for each initiative, we tentatively distributed the implementation actions across the appropriate functions. Finally, we developed a plan to communicate the new short-term initiatives, the impact and timing we expected, and the respective assignments, to the broader organization.

"Now, let's talk about how we're going to pass along this information to all of the folks who report to each of you. I would really appreciate some suggestions."

"They will see some of what we're proposing as having been tried before," Maria warned. "To avoid having them tune out, we need to come up with some fresh expressions or examples or ways of explaining our goals. Same-ol', same-ol' isn't going to hack it."

"You're exactly right, Maria," I concurred. "But can you give me an example of how we can present this approach that is perceived as redundant in a new way."

"I'll have to think a little more about that," Maria responded.

"I once read a passage by **Ron Ashkenas** and **Rizwan Khan** that summarized our situation pretty well:"

"The announcement is the easy part; it makes the manager look bold and decisive. Implementation is more difficult, because no matter how good and compelling the data, there will always be active and passive resistance, rationalizations, debates, and distractions— particularly when the changes require new ways of working or painful cuts. To get through this, managers have to get their hands dirty, engage their teams to make choices, and sometimes confront recalcitrant colleagues."

"How about by doing instead of talking," I said. "You know the old adage about actions speaking louder than words. In realigning a business, that's especially true. So, yes, we've got to sell our coworkers on the reality that we've carefully thought through these changes. As well, we'll need to demonstrate to them that we're under pressure regarding the time we have to accomplish this turnaround and generate success. Lectures, pep talks, and warnings aren't going to be effective. We very simply need to be involved and walk the talk."

Maria grinned and said, "You want us to convey to them that our message is that they should do as we do."

I nodded. "That's part of it, but not all. We need to do things differently. First, we need to lead by example. So, right now, I want each of you to write out one resolution regarding a behavior of yours that you will commit to changing as a clear example of how everyone is going to have to put the company's needs first."

"I'd like to quit smoking." quipped Dick.

"I'm referring to a management behavior." My tone accepted his kidding. "Look down at the notes you've been taking all day. Focus on something significant. Off the top of my head, I'd say a good resolution for you might be to discuss any major order with the rest of the team before you commit to a due date."

Dick squinted. "We've tried that before, and I've never gotten a decent response in time to give the customer an answer when they need it. What's gonna change that?"

"New thinking and team commitment!" I insisted. "Okay, so from today on, the rest of the team and I will commit to a twenty-four-hour response to any customer request. Will that work?"

Dick nodded somewhat skeptically, but Geoff and Janet squirmed a bit.

"But that isn't enough; we need to broaden it so each one of us has a commitment that can affect the behaviors of the others on our teams. Maria, what might the HR team offer as a behavioral change that will help our improvement efforts?"

"I'm thinking we'll need to try and accelerate our on-boarding process for factory employees."

"Do we have a lot of turnover, and if so, are our wage and benefit packages competitive?" I responded.

"We've lost people in the past over surprisingly small things. Although we subscribe to local surveys for wages and benefits and are competitive, we could be more responsive at resolving employee concerns."

"Can you cover both in the on-boarding process? Say, with early employment satisfaction surveys?" I pressed her a little.

"I think we can, yes. I'm willing to take a shot at that goal."

"John! How about you?" I was perhaps getting a little boisterous now.

"I would like to introduce a *fast track* for simple orders that allow us to move it through our systems and on to operations in one day." He replied.

"Nice! Put together a plan and lets all review it!" My enthusiasm was growing. "Jolene?"

"Well, I'm not too sure what finance can change. We have as many outside obligations as we do internal ones."

"I have a request then." I gave her a quick smile. "I would like you to construct a daily impact report that feeds the entire staff updates on changes in orders, shipments, inventory, and workforce spending. It will give us all timely insight as to how we're doing."

"Sure. I'll be by to discuss it later." She was visibly concerned about the "*how*" to get that done.

"Janet and Geoff! I would like the two of you to work with Dick and come up with a list of inventory *bets.* From there we'll determine what products to place the bets on in order to reduce response time."

Geoff spoke quickly. "I think you will need to be involved in that exercise, because there will be considerable disagreement amongst us as to what actions we should be taking."

"Okay, I'll break the ties, but you three will need to come together and give me a proposal first. Then we can go from there!"

At least in theory, we were all headed in the same direction.

Lead with Vision

Even great organizations can fail to address major problems in their business because of an inability to identify the causes and focus on corrective measures. I think, sometimes, it's because these organizations fear that undertaking a major improvement effort might compromise an already tenuous status quo. It seems as if they are playing defense, trying hard to not lose rather than striving to win. They diligently attack symptoms as if they're independent events, or separate causes, rather than recognizing them as the consequences of deeper problems. These actions cause them to employ insufficient solutions that can create even more trouble. For example, adding an approval step for material procurement as a measure of inventory reduction. The real problem is more likely either broken forecasting or glitches in the ordering process. But rather than correct the process problem, imposing a containment style oversight step is faster and seems harmless. The truth is that it usually serves to dull the response time of the whole business as people wait for approvals, compounding the problem rather than correcting it. More often than not, these moves force people to work around the system, breaking things down even further. When attempts to correct a problem actually degrade performance, possibly incurring another ill-thought-out response that degrades things *even* further, we call this phenomenon the "death spiral."

1. Situation Assessment: Looking *into* instead of around

There is a fine line between vision and hallucination, and the only difference is a plan! I say this often to stress that no matter how far-fetched a vision might appear, if it can be rooted in reality through careful and diligent planning, then it can be transformed from a fantasy into something achievable. It's important to understand that the attainability of an objective is a key factor in associate engagement. Translating a vision into an executable plan allows leaders to walk on the correct side of that fine line and when presented to associates, plays a factor in whether or not they will follow. I use a combination of techniques to understand the current state of every organization I participate in and use the observations to establish an early level of reality. Establishing this base is always optimum for setting "stretch" objectives that are truly achievable.

- *Reconnoitering*: An old pathfinders' term that refers to the practice of using multiple benchmarks within one's surroundings to approximate a current location and to determine the correct direction to start. In business, reconnoitering equates to stepping back from the current action in order to gain a broader view of your entire surroundings. "Walk" the business and observe its visual indicators—both good and bad. This will help you assemble a rough list of things that need to change and a list of things that should be left alone. Remember, though, that what you can see are only symptoms, and their root causes are likely camouflaged and harder to uncover. Update your list regularly and modify it as often as necessary in order to fine tune your course of improvement.

- *Triangulation*: While it's senior leadership's responsibility to establish a vision for the business, rooting that plan in reality requires a thorough situation assessment. Triangulation between the current performance of the business, your competitors' performance, and the known market benchmarks for customer expectations will yield an assessment that is more securely based in fact. Determining the coordinates of the business amidst these three points can identify the standard for performance excellence and help to reveal any gaps that will need a strategy for closure. Once it's defined, translating these points into a vision that challenges the organization to pursue what's possible, while at the same time stretching it toward a set of breakthrough objectives, becomes a highly credible task supported by three legs of reality.

- *Alignment*. An organization will inherently sense the difference between vision and hallucination. When the goals, execution plans, and deployment all fail to line up with one another, it creates a lack of believability that blurs the clarity of your vision and must be corrected before commitment or buy-in can be sought. Oftentimes, even when the details are well-defined, the attainability of stretched objectives will fail to be clear to your associates without some additional definition and salesmanship. Just like a tree, the loftiness of a company's growth is controlled by the depths of its roots. The ability to reach high objectives is limited by how well grounded the logic and supporting information for the vision are. This information not only forms the basis for a set of newly established goals, it serves as an outline for communicating its purpose.

- *A 360° View*. No matter how your initiatives get started, it's essential that the vision be woven from a blend of *external drivers* (markets and competitors) and *internal needs* (closing performance gaps). In history, a good example of a lack of vision is the construction of the Maginot Line, a series of fixed battlements built by France on its border with Germany in the years following World War I. The French designed the wall to keep the Germans from overrunning them in any future war, but the strategy was flawed because it focused on war tactics in their current state at the end of World War One, failing to consider how they might evolve with future changes in technology and tactics. By the time the defenses were completed, new technologies (tanks and planes) and their related battle tactics had already evolved in a way that effectively made fortressed walls obsolete. When World War II broke out, the Germans made an easy task of flying over and blasting through the defenses, quickly capitulating the French. The lesson: A correct vision not only attends to the current state but is actively adjusted to adapt to future needs as well. It must anticipate new challenges and seize current opportunities if it's to be capable of withstanding assault by technologies that may not exist in the present.

2. Defining Your Vision: Visualize a path that can be followed

Your organizational vision is your "case for change" and can originate from something as simple as a high-level philosophical statement, or it can be built using a team-based tactical exercise. For example, stating something like, "We would like to become the market leader" is similar, but different from, "We need to move ourselves from the middle tier to the top tier of our competitive peer group." Though both can mean relatively the same thing, the latter suggests the presence of more substance. No matter how it's worded, your vision statement must offer a sufficient amount of credibility to suggest that the vision itself makes sense. A business may have a vision to become the market leader, or to move its perceived identity upmarket from that of a "component parts maker" into a "systems integrator," but any vision's objective should be realistic enough to appear attainable, whether it's intended to be the result of a strategy or one of evolution. At times this may necessitate breaking the macro-vision into smaller micro-steps. Creating a rational and functional vision requires the correct basis data, substantial preparatory work, and a logical execution plan.

- *Untouchables*: A key step in framing the vision begins by having the leadership team define those existing principles within the organization that cannot be altered. These will include elements that make up the current state, such as a market-leading product quality; a tradition of exemplary customer service, market or brand value elements; business ethics and personal morality; and possibly even the brand logo or mission statement. Why are these chosen elements untouchable? If they are significant enough to form some of the value of the current business, they should also be foundational in its transformation to a future state. Even more important, their continuity serves as a stable vantage point from which people can stay connected to the principles that factored into their earlier success. In a turnaround, this can avert employee despair that nothing they had ever done was right and everything needs to be fixed. The reality is that there are always plenty of other things to change, so it's unwise to tackle anything that isn't broken. Save your time and resources for the true needs of the business. The bottom line is that the leader who comes in and believes everything should be changed is probably wrong.

- *Must Changes*: With the untouchables defined, the list of critical changes becomes clearer and easier to identify: improvement of competitive position or core competencies, new product development and launch, and possibly even order management and fulfillment. All of these are capable of transforming business performance, elevating market position, or building brand integrity. They're also in line with the achievement of the visionary objectives. Once each factor is evaluated for priority and potential impact, they will collectively comprise the must-change list that serves as the foundation for an overarching strategy. As the must-change list is drafted, recheck it against the untouchables to make sure that none pose a barrier for progress. Such conflicts should be resolved carefully in order to preserve the most important elements from each list.

- *Integration.* Translating your vision into an executable strategy is a far more tactical step that should enlist the broader organization, helping to build buy-in, enhancing organizational skills, and ensuring that all valid input is considered. Objectives for growth, profitability, or market share should be based on market information, customer feedback, business performance, benchmarking information, and even the organizations culture. Having the team "mine" this detail helps create the "roots" that ground the vision in their eyes, preventing it from degrading into a hallucination. The facts and data used to connect the vision to reality also formulate a basis for communication during deployment to the organization.

- *Clarity*: To better understand the need to provide clarity of purpose, consider one company whose vision came from the top in the form of a corporate mantra, along with a non-negotiable, assigned "percentage of improvement task" over a strategic planning period of three years. The business unit teams set improvement targets for both the programs and their metrics that were based upon the prior year's performance and in line with the corporate objectives. Because the corporation's annual plans were always structured as the first-year stepping stone leading toward achievement of the three-year strategic plan (adjusted annually based on actual attainment as well as for market changes), the resultant metric targets provided a pace of progress that enabled its achievement. Although a top-down approach may seem to be an arguable methodology, the results were never in doubt. The improvement task was woven into tightly-linked planning processes covering strategy adjustments, business cycle targets, and organizational development that consistently stretched the enterprise. This company consistently achieved significant improvements, in large part because they so tightly integrated their planning and execution efforts and grounded their improvement targets with their baselines. The involvement and discipline built into the execution and follow-up became the differentiator. The key lesson here is: "If your team can visualize a path, they will be more willing to follow it."

3. **Communicate the Vision: Inform and Sell to Build Excitement, Engage to Generate Buy-in.**

Once it's developed, the final step is to communicate the vision. Although your primary motive is to energize the rest of the organization by communicating this information, this should be held until the last step in the process. Pushing an implementation plan forward without preparing the team for the news can have divisive results that might impede buy-in and delay progress.

- *Inform*: Providing the appropriate information is the first step in successful communication. Bring the team up to speed on the facts supporting the vision, what's required, and why it's necessary. Most people will buy into a better future, so the vision should target something better, more concrete. "Rooting your vision in reality" uses the lens of attainability to build credibility. A vision that entails stretch objectives won't automatically make sense to everyone, but if a competitor has already blazed a trail to similar achievements, the organization's need to meet or improve upon their competitive achievements helps ground it—regardless of how far it stretches them from their current position. A memorable example of this was the message delivered by President Kennedy when he communicated the challenge of the space race in the early 1960s. The Soviets had already cracked the atmosphere, establishing a sort of technical precedent. JFK set a timeline that was long enough (by the end of the decade) to minimize the "impossibility factor," making the goal of placing a man on the moon seem plausible. His administrators at NASA may not have initially bought into this timeline, but I'm certain that once it was set, they took comfort in the amount of time they had to find a way. The key reason for doing the groundwork and for taking care in structuring and staging the communication is to accomplish buy-in. The less plausible the objective, the stronger the roots will have to be.

- *Relate*: The next step in communicating the vision is to sell it and build excitement. Start by using two levels of communication to achieve a more favorable impact. The first and most important level explains how it will positively impact individual concerns: employees need to see what's in it for them. The message needs to be inclusive enough to apply to everyone, yet diverse enough to address each functional group in the organization. The second level covers the favorable benefits to the business itself. It's wise to translate the implementation plan into a favorable benefit for each specific area of the business, and then package them to show the benefits to the overall business. This helps to cover any concerns of "what's in it for me" as well as "what's in it for all of us" components.

- *Involve*: Step three for engaging people in the vision is to describe how they will be affected. Helping them understand how their input will shape both the results and outcome, as well as where the vision might be adjusted to accommodate their inclusion will aid in the development of credibility. Make these descriptions general enough to touch everyone by first stopping them at the functional objective level and then separating them from the more specific group and individual objectives. This degree of "trickle down" is adequate for this stage of the process.

- *Focus*: It takes all three elements of communication to get everyone focused on the vision. As the communication process is initiated, there are certain pitfalls to avoid. First, never assume that just because a message has been delivered that it has been comprehended. To achieve understanding, make your messages simple, direct, genuine, and confine them to essential elements. Doing so reduces tension and relieves anxiety. Second, the communications must be timely. Get word out well in advance of initial start-ups so that no one is caught off-guard or made to feel out of the loop. Staying ahead of the rumor mill will enhance the credibility of the communication. The messages should state the game plan directly, delineate the timetable, and identify the benefits to everyone involved (management, employees, customers, stockholders). Building organizational commitment to the strategy and its implementation are critical elements of success; enabling the leadership team to walk the talk and keep the path to success less steep, making it easier for associates to follow.

- *Continuity*: Implementing a new vision requires adjusting the list of tactical programs that are currently consuming resources. As the transitional strategies are identified, all existing tactical activities that can support the new vision should be retained, while new tactical requirements should be identified, initiated, and monitored for their contribution to success. The sustained activities help keep the amount of change more manageable, easing adaptability and strengthening morale. All tactical programs that no longer apply to the strategy should be deferred or discontinued in order to better focus the team on the new direction, a difficult but essential step to free up resources. Having integrated both sets of actions, timing can be applied to the tactical objective set.

In the 1400s Niccolo Machiavelli wrote, "It ought to be remembered that there is nothing more difficult to take in hand, more perilous to conduct, or more uncertain in its success, than to take the lead in the introduction of a new order of things." He was right, and although Machiavelli's mandates, as recorded in *The Prince*, are often dark, blunt, harsh, and uncompromising, his words quite often have application to 21st century business matters, for he also adds, "The innovator has for enemies all those who have done well under the old conditions, and lukewarm defenders in those who will do well under the new."

A more current interpretation of Machiavelli's words would suggest that in order to reduce resistance to change, it's necessary to convince as many colleagues and associates as possible of the potential benefits the changes will provide. Otherwise, folks will maintain comfort with what they already know, the normal routine, or, simply put, same "stuff" different day. Clearly stating the expected results, outlining the methods to be used, and ensuring their involvement in the change process will go a long way toward reducing the fear of the unknown. These are the steps that sharpen your hallucination into a clear vision, allowing for support and success.

In the coming chapters, we'll explore ways to put the new strategy to work so as to generate results quickly and maximize efforts. In the meantime, it's important to remember that adjustments to your leadership approach are required in order to facilitate the development, deployment, and execution of a winning strategy for the business. It is ultimately the executive leader's "Response-Ability" to show the team the way.

Chapter 2: Leadership Response-Ability

Setting the tone for a more Responsive Organization.

2.1 Align for Response

2.2 Securing a "Confession of Reality"

2.3 Motivating the Organization

2.4 Work Enterprise-Wide

2.5 Design Your Processes

2.6 Creating Organizational Focus

The entire organization had stepped up to the challenge of containing the critical business issues, and we were starting to see some results. After only three months, most customers had taken notice of our improvements in delivery and response, and several of them had started to increase their orders, though still a bit wary about the sustainability of our rejuvenated performance. Indeed, while many of our internal systemic problems had been contained or solved, a handful of noisome issues still remained that would require more extensive work.

However, we had earned enough breathing room over the day-to-day issues to allow us to shift our focus toward looking for more strategic solutions to some of our greater challenges. It was time to take advantage of the respite and invite the senior staff, along with their direct reports, to an offsite strategy review. I wanted to elevate their line of sight from the tactical tasks at hand toward those long-term actions that would really impact our performance. In preparation, they were asked to assemble all of the available market intelligence, product and service development priorities, and operating performance information into a review format for the team.

"First, I'd like to make everyone aware that our performance improvements have encouraged three of our largest customers to remove us from probationary status and reward us with two new orders." The room filled with applause.

"Although I know you all realize how beneficial that is, thus far we've accomplished everything by lifting ourselves up by our own bootstraps. Our results have improved more through muscle than finesse, and because that isn't a recipe for sustainability, we'll need to develop long-term solutions. As we discuss our business strategy today for the first time together, I want you to think about our options for turning the business from survival, to excellence, to growth. For now, think about issues and processes rather than actions. Believe me, actions will come later."

With that, Dick stepped up front. "I've been asked to put the customer first, so we'll start there. By now everyone knows that our customer base is highly frustrated with our inability to deliver to our commitments, and although they will tell you our quality is acceptable, the truth is, it could be better. Let's look at how we compare to our competitors."

He put up a few graphs with competitive data showing some industry information for product quality and delivery, before finishing with our pricing position in the market. "I don't want you to draw any conclusions about this yet. For example, it's okay to be the most expensive, as long as the product and service levels you offer justify it from a value perspective."

Maria stepped up next. "I would like to inform you about our organizational structure and staffing, as well as the recruitment plans, we have in place. In doing so, we need to be open to the possible need to make adjustments to get us in line with our new strategy." She went through the individual team charts, and talked a bit about how it linked to the prior operating strategy, before proceeding into a short chat about the culture.

When Maria finished, John stepped up front. "Our objectives for engineering are much more basic: Reduce our turnaround time for product customization, and begin a platform strategy to modularize our system offerings. This is going to take some effort, and we won't be able to just add people, at least not at the beginning."

Janet was next. "From a supply chain perspective, we'll need to develop more favorable agreements with our key suppliers when it comes to lead time and inventory position. It also means we'll have to develop a forecasting model, and 'place some bets' on where we think we might be able to add inventory and improve our market performance."

The rest of the functional leaders or their direct reports offered similar information related to their own areas. After they finished, we took a short break.

With the presentations complete and their minds refreshed a bit, we re-convened into four smaller groups, each led by a staff member along with an independent facilitator I had brought in for the specific purpose of getting everyone to think less tactically and more "big picture." The team assignments were to develop an analysis of our Strengths, Weaknesses, Opportunities, and Threats (also called a SWOT) for the business as a whole. For the most part, these reviews are heavily based on opinion, however, there was sufficient data provided by the staff presentations to support them. When the SWOTs were complete, team leaders presented them to the group for discussion and as a starting point to develop a consensus on ranking their importance, as well as to identify potential countermeasures.

As we entered the SWOT review, there were clear disagreements between members of the groups as to what each list should contain, and these had found their way into the individual chart discussions. I asked Dick to lead the discussion with the "strengths" team, and as I stood back and only observed, but it quickly became obvious that achieving a true consensus would be challenging.

"I think our customer service processes are a strength," the team leader for customer service spoke up. "If they weren't, the way our orders get messed up, we wouldn't have any business left."

"I certainly think the breadth of our product offerings is a strength. We will do things our competitors won't, and it wins us sales," one of the Sales managers said.

Next, I moved to the "Weaknesses" team, to observe their conversations.

"Our product offerings are so broad, they bind up our operations and prevent us from delivering on time," one of the production managers said. Clearly, he wasn't within ear shot of the strengths group.

Both of the other two teams, Opportunities and Threats, were having similar conflicts throughout their discussions. As I stopped by to observe each, I could sense some tension.

After the groups completed their full cycle of the four areas of the SWOT, its output provided us some additional "ground level" information (a combination of market-supported facts and experiential opinions) to suggest a new direction for the business and the need to act quickly. We still needed to blend that list with the prescriptive elements of our parent corporations' strategy to complete the organizational objectives and set the stage for their translation into both short and long-range goals. With that completed, the meeting was adjourned to give the senior staff time to rewrite the master list of possible strategic initiatives emanating from the SWOTs, and put together a priority assessment, some suggested countermeasures, and weave in the list of mandatory corporate initiatives.

For our second session, we expanded the participants to include key next-level functional, technical, and customer leaders. Their mission was to challenge the strategic initiatives identified by the senior staff before helping to translate them into a more detailed set of attainment projects. We asked them to hold nothing sacred—not previous performance paradigms or constraining business processes; all were subject to change once we established the final set of priorities.

"Good morning!" I could hardly contain my enthusiasm as I addressed the team. So far, we were making great progress and had identified some transformational initiatives along the way. "Welcome to the second round of our strategic development process. By the end of today, we'll have put a framework to a new business strategy. As a team, our job today is to ensure that this plan is comprehensive, grounded, plainly stated, and supported by a complete list of projects and metrics by which to gauge our progress. When I say comprehensive, it must include both critical customer-facing goals, along with substantial improvements to our business performance and culture. Following the customer objectives will be operational performance, product initiatives, business process, and financial goals—organized in the order of greatest impact. While it should have stretch objectives, they should also be attainable. Once we've defined everything, we will use a process called Strategy Deployment to put it into action as soon as we can communicate it to the organization."

"How much of this has been dictated to us from corporate?" a senior engineering associate asked.

"Honestly, there are a couple of corporate projects and some target financial metrics that are provided for us, but the rest is for us to determine. The staff and I took an initial stab at it last month, so your role will be both to challenge our view, and to help us build it into an achievable plan."

Each staff member was asked to introduce his or her "champion" for their particular initiative. As a staff, we'd built a list of nominees that we reached consensus on, to help determine suitability. All of the incumbents were developmental leadership candidates with considerable career "runway."

As we unveiled the draft of organizational initiatives to the team, there appeared to be a sense of relief to those in the room. It seemed to be a clear indication that the staff's draft initiatives list was very close to what the group believed would be necessary to turn the business around.

"Please let me remind you that this list of objectives we're showing you is absolutely preliminary and that our mission for this meeting is to fine-tune and eventually finalize the list. Your participation and contributions are necessary and greatly appreciated. I will stress again that there are no boundaries for any suggested solutions at this time, you need to dream a bit."

"One of your financial goals is to improve margins. Does this mean we will be raising prices?" a regional sales manager asked.

"That wouldn't be my first choice because it's usually self-defeating. I would rather say that we will first deal with operational inefficiencies, and as we roll them up, see if we can accomplish our goals that way. Another approach may be to develop some high margin options." That response seemed to satisfy the questioner, and the room became quiet.

With a pause in the question-and-answer opening, I turned the discussion in another direction. "Now I'd like to talk to you about 'Response-Ability,' and not the one-word kind." A slide with the crossed-out word "responsibility" was placed on the screen. "Rather, my version looks like this." A second slide with "Response-Ability" popped up in front of them. "I use this version to convey that it's my duty as a leader of this business to be responsive to customer needs *WITHIN the same timing that the fulfillment of those needs is expected by THEM*. My job is to maintain these internal relationships so that they are constantly functional and continuously improving. This is *my* Response-Ability, and it will be a key theme for all of us moving forward. Each and every one of you as associates in this organization must accept the responsibility of fulfilling the customer needs in the timing they expect, not necessarily in the timing we are capable of. Further, this responsibility will find its way into our process designs to ensure that each and every operational and business process can respond within the response time basis required by our respective markets."

"But how do we relate non-operational processes like Human Resources, or Accounting to response time?" Jolene asked. Although we had discussed this as a staff, she wanted to make certain that everyone in the room understood the concept.

"My view is that every function and process in our business has a linkage to, our product and services response, either directly or indirectly. When we move into redefining our operating metrics, we will find those linkages and establish them as the 'time' metric for each function or process. Thanks for that question Jolene; more to come. It's now time to turn the customer facing part of the discussion over to Dick."

"Now, I'd like all of us to talk about our present customer relationships." Dick began. "Let's review the data we have from every customer touch-point, including direct metrics and tangible interpersonal feedback. As you do this, we should strive to place ourselves in our customers' shoes in order to more objectively view how we perform. If you were our customer, what would *you* expect from us?"

We embarked on a lengthy discussion of our present customer relationships, with the customer-facing functions setting the stage by communicating some facts along with direct feedback about our performance. His team then reviewed some higher-level market forecast information along with some current technological trends. Dick reminded them of the need for everyone to maintain a clear "line of sight" on both the current and future customer needs by building them in as a goal for each organizational initiative. That was the best way to keep our goals from being overly internalized.

"Now that we have explored the customer perspective from our own view—what *we* think *they* think; I'm going to ask you to take a quick lunch break. After lunch we'll have Paul Johnson, CEO of Valhalla Product Solutions Inc., give us his perspective on our performance." The group quickly dispersed.

When we reconvened, I introduced Mr. Johnson.

"Greetings, everyone, it's an honor to be here" he began. "When I was initially asked to come and speak to you, I was concerned about how negative the message was going to be. To be quite frank, you were doing so poorly that we were planning to replace you as one of our key suppliers. When we benchmarked you against other market competitors, neither your ability to respond nor the quality of the incoming products measured up to our or, for that matter, our industry's standards. Because your performance was impacting our own business in a negative way, we felt that you were leaving us no choice but to seek alternative supply. That said, while your recent progress is encouraging, you should also be aware that we can't yet trust that you've fully corrected all of the problems and that we will continue to explore other supply options on a parallel path"

He carefully articulated his view of our performance, the areas where he felt we needed to focus our efforts, and the level of progress necessary to maintain our present level of business. I was somewhat comforted to hear that his impressions of what we needed to accomplish were largely in line with those we had identified in our own discussions.

"How much time do we have to fix it?" Dick asked, offering the perfect setup question, probably because they knew each other so well.

"I would say you will need to be a level just below world-class performance within the next year. Please recognize that the market is constantly raising the bar on you, so the target you set today may be too low for tomorrow. I can also assure you that the penalty for failure will be sudden and severe."

His timeline was much shorter than we had imagined, and I could sense that his bluntly dire prediction of consequence was somewhat unnerving to many of those in the room. He completed his remarks and followed with some casual questions and answers before departing. As we walked together to his rental car, I thanked him for his message and assured him that it would be taken with the gravity in which it was delivered. His perspective helped greatly in setting the tone for the balance of the day's efforts.

Startled and with a more urgent perspective of our key customer's point of view, the team proceeded to their cross-functional working groups with the task of drafting the implementation game plan for these new initiatives, providing substance to the vision. The deliverables for this exercise included a description of the objective, a clear definition of the metrics of success, identifying functional ownership along with assigning an initiative champion, and, finally, the list of projects necessary for success. Once each team completed this work on their initiative, the teams came back together as a group to review, critique, and provide input—fine tuning what that earlier team had established. The process sequence continued until each initiative had been reviewed and the individual goal established.

By this point, the benefits of the session were beginning to become more obvious to the team. Collaboration was already improving, and it was providing solutions that had a more cross-functional flair. The objectives and projects they had identified and prioritized were difficult, but capable of delivering rapid improvement. Also, a broadened sense of commitment to deliver the improved results was developing. Much of the confidence in attainability stemmed from matching the objectives and metric targets to the market needs, rather than just using incremental targets or a "dartboard" methodology—throwing ideas at the board to see what sticks. Each participant was starting to envision a better result.

"I truly appreciate all of your engagement and participation in this process. Our next task will be to communicate an understandable high-level version of the strategy to the rest of the organization. Sarah Clayton once said, 'Few things are more important during a change event than communication from leaders who can paint a clear and confidence-inspiring vision of the future.'

"This will take a team effort from all of us. We'll need to solicit our associates' support in filling out the broader project team assignments before kicking off the work. Does anyone have any questions?"

"I'd like to know how we intend to approach the product platform initiative. It's honestly a huge project that could take years." One engineering team leader asked.

"I'll defer to John for that answer."

"We'll seek the opinion of the market along with some of our business imperatives to establish our priorities," John replied. "Then we'll figure out how to take it one step at a time. I've already given it a lot of thought, and have some ideas I'll want to run by all of you"

Since all of the individuals responsible for managing the entire organization were in the room, I asked them to give some thought as to how they would allocate resources for the new programs, as well as solve the need for project leadership, the transition of existing programs onto the project list, and the possibility of the need to eliminate or shelve noncritical programs. These would all have to be addressed before attempting to communicate the strategy to the greater organization.

Though the term, "Leadership Response-Ability" was introduced in the opening chapter, let's look at the definition that the term was created convey. I wanted it to define leadership that is responsive to the needs of an organization, with a sense of timing and an intense focus that satisfies those needs. But, how do you define that need for response?

Every market has competitive forces that help to define the response requirements in which its participants must provide products or services to a specific customer base. The providers "response model" must be designed to meet the market requirements in a time frame that makes him competitive in that market. Stated more plainly, if you sell products from a shelf, then you must be able to replace a unit of product as quickly as one sells. If you manufacture products to order and advertise an eight-week order fulfillment time, then your materials acquisition and manufacturing systems must be designed to enable an eight-week response even when demand changes. Because this timing requirement is market-defined, it also necessarily applies to every peripheral support activity that affects fulfillment: decision timing, organizational objectives, and metrics management. Fulfilling your "Leadership Response-Ability" requires you to integrate this market timing into your management review processes in order to develop and maintain a culture whose own responsiveness is in line with the needs of its market and the business as a whole.

Aligning for Response: Diagnose the Culture

But how do you establish this type of responsiveness in an organization that doesn't possess it? First, you'll need to determine the response timing requirements present in the market that the business serves. They may be different depending upon the complexity of the business itself (multiple markets, etc.). The starting point is to define *takt*, a German word for the baton that an orchestra director uses to control the tempo of the performance. In *Lean Enterprise, Takt* is used to refer to the "rhythm of the market," and is typically converted into time: Takt Time. Although the application of *takt/takt time* has typically been reserved for the manufacture of end-item goods or services and the capacity to produce them, it should also be used to define the cadence that applies to business processes. Using conversions of takt time will enable you to utilize your own market rhythms to drive all of your business activities, better linking them to results. Aligning everything you do around the cadence of a businesses end deliverable is just a smart thing to do.

In order to build that timing (or segments of that timing) into your business processes, start with your review cycles because reviewing your performance, process, or metrics too infrequently may prevent you from taking timely corrective action on problems, causing performance erosion. Conversely, reviewing them too frequently will waste valuable time. A great place to start is with your program and metrics reviews. They will typically have some discipline already associated with them and it's relatively easy to tie their timing to expectations of behavior.

Finally, you'll need to introduce sustainable methodologies to help you stick to the disciplines, refine them, and constantly confirm their alignment with the customer base. We'll take a more in-depth look at these in chapters 6 and 10, but, for now, you'll want to perform a deployment check in order to maximize the involvement of your organization. Close it out with a periodic improvement review and you will turn process performance information into improvement actions.

To be truly effective in driving the implementation, be sure to utilize your leadership team's understanding of the organizations culture. Personalizing the pace and content of your communications to the organization will increase acceptance, engagement, and ultimately speed your success!

Secure a "Confession of Reality": Engage your leadership skills to develop an understanding of how the organization moves and breathes, and then translate it into targeted action.

As a leader, it's always helpful to remember that both patience and impatience are essential components of your management style. Patience is a foremost style characteristic that will encourage people to follow you, and demonstrating a measured approach to managing change is less intimidating. But to be honest, it's the judicious use of impatience that provides a fundamental leveraging tool for the call to action. So, while both are essential, striking a balance with a bias slightly in favor of patience will allow people to become more comfortable with your management style and still allow you to impart an appropriate sense of urgency to your change initiative.

Steering the leadership team toward a confession of reality takes more patience. When you're trying to get team leaders to admit to the current state of a struggling business, using impatience will only scare them into a false reading. Self-admission is a powerful tool for generating buy-in both to the problem and the solutions, but it requires tremendous finesse to steer them away from assigning responsibility (often referred to as blame). The alignment of a mutual reality (for the businesses and associates) with a basic desire to go forward and improve it, is an important enabler for people to understand the need for change.

The SWOT analysis is a great tool to unearth that reality. Properly conducted, it can clearly identify all four aspects (Strengths, Weaknesses, Opportunities, and Threats) that will need to be addressed by the strategy. Great care must be taken however to support the opinions of the participants with factual basis, the primary reason a SWOT should be preceded with a thorough business and market performance data.

Identify Embedded Behaviors

Understanding the responsive behaviors in an organization and getting people to admit to and accept the need to improve the current state are the first two steps needed to begin a cultural diagnostic. There are a couple of additional perspectives that should be examined before attempting to change a culture. You should always try and ascertain an organization's culture by taking the time to first observe the embedded behaviors internally and then by assessing the internal and external influences that tend to move it. After that you can move on the motivations it is responsive to.

The first behavioral or cultural trait to define is **organizational focus**. This simply involves the way associates go about the tasks they are engaged in at the time you begin to contemplate your change initiative. It's easiest to just walk around and ask people what they spend most of their time doing. Don't look for a detailed explanation as much as just a general idea of the type of activities they're engaged in. Is it related to an active project? Are they off on a tangent—a project, legitimate or otherwise, that isn't in the objective set? Are they trying to get containment over some kind of problem—putting out fires? A complex answer is much better than an "I don't know," but neither is particularly good. Lack of focus will strand work in-process short of completion, while intense mono-focus can often leave other necessary activities unattended. I once had responsibility for a facility whose culture was described by an outsider as "ants at a picnic." The observer was telling me that any time an issue popped up, everyone ran to it. Unfortunately, that behavior occurred without real priority, causing numerous important projects to be interrupted or dropped, often preventing them from taking problems to closure and gaining ground in the bigger picture.

The next critical behavioral attribute is **responsiveness**. Culturally, this can range from either an organization that puts its customers first (very good), to one which looks at its customer expectations with a sort of disdain, making excuses as to why personal issues or internal business matters are more important (very bad) than the satisfaction of market needs that they consider inherently flawed. A responsive culture intrinsically understands that whereas its customers aren't necessarily always right, they are always their customers, and it's they who keep cash flowing in. As such, customer needs should always take priority over internal issues. I can't tell you how many times I've entered an organization where the internal attitude was that the customers never know what they want, and because of that, "their emergency is not ours," so we'll put them in line and get to them when we can! Unfortunately, being able to respond to any customer needs in their timeframe is an opportunity to set yourself apart from your competitors, and building a capability that enables you to do so cost effectively can be an integral strategy to win over marginal markets. The most successful businesses have redefined their own markets through responsiveness (think Amazon). Customers settle matters with their feet, or sometimes today online—if dissatisfied, they may leave and never return.

A third vitally important cultural behavior is **adaptability**, and it too can be a mixed blessing! Excessive adaptability might create an organization that eschews standardization and makes consistency difficult to achieve. While all organizations require a certain number of standards, set procedures, and well-controlled practices to ensure reliable delivery of products and services, those processes cannot be so constraining as to rigidify response. An inflexible attitude that limits your ability to accommodate those occasional out-of-the-ordinary customer requests will label you as a company that's too rigid to be counted upon in emergencies or too staid to co-develop new product new offerings with. Properly balanced, your company should be able to have a stabilized structure and delivery processes that are reliable, but that also have exceptional management contingencies for suggestions, alteration requests, and product improvements. Without process stability, there can be no consistency of performance; without sufficient adaptability, there can be no improvement, acquisition of new markets, or advancement in areas such as research and development, key requisites for growth.

Communication is the final embedded cultural behavior that should be understood up front. Organizations that don't communicate well tend to be functionally isolated, causing a failure to work effectively between departments, ultimately forming "silos." The visible existence of any type of timely, disciplined communications moving between levels and across functions, either through periodic reviews and/or general information sessions, is a great indicator of a company's commitment to communications.

The chart below demonstrates how these four behaviors inter-relate to define a company culture, affect customer relationships, and potentially impair the ability to drive change. It further suggests that a balanced culture will most readily accept and adapt to a change initiative.

Benchmarking Culture	Organizational Result				
Cultural Descriptor	"Ants at a Picnic"	At the Brink of Overload	"Masters of Execution"	Bored Underachievers	"Drones"
Customer Satisfaction Level	Low	Satisfied	Highly Satisfied	Satisfied	Low
Organizational Focus	Focus Deficit - many activities without priorities, no discipline to finish in process activities.	Too many priorities, some focus but prioritization is lacking	Focus is organized along key initiative execution, priorities are clear, achievement level is high	Minimal activities or priorities, very focused	Intense mono-focus - very few initiatives in process.
Responsiveness	Ultra High Sense of Urgency - Frenetic	High urgency, over reactive	Highly responsive	Responsive when pressed	No urgency - Organization is generally non-responsive outside of standard procedures
Adaptability	Highly adaptive - nothing is standard, customization is not controlled	Adaptive - few standards, excessive customization	Timely adaptation to market changes - Standards are leveraged and customization is controlled	Limited adaptability, very standardized, customizes when forced	Not adaptive - Everything is standard - nothing is customized
Communications	Excessive communications - Can't keep up or meaningless	Communication level is high, but value is low	Timely-clear communication of org. goals and progress	Some structured communications, value is low	Minimal to no communications - doesn't generate interest (apathy)
Rate of Change	Resistant	Constant	Controlled	Inconsistent	Resistant

Discovering your "Spheres of Influence"

In my own management career, I've learned that every organization has one or two aspects, sometimes called functions or disciplines, which assert an overriding influence on the others. Most of the time it comes from the long-term effects of having multiple senior leaders of the same ilk: Sales, Accounting, Operations, etc.

In every company, these subsets of the organization possess significantly more authority than the rest. The basis for their influence can originate both externally (e.g., customers or regulatory) and internally (individuals or organizational subsets), and they play a huge role in defining its culture. Sometimes finding them is as easy as looking to the most senior leader to see which group he originated from or confides in the most, or look for where the authority who provides approval resides. Once you've identified these cultural influencers, you can gain a greater understanding of what drives them by looking at how they align themselves to exert force. Three primary factors generate cultural influence, so I've arranged them into spheres, with variable overlaps to depict a specific emphasis. The proper arrangement of these spheres should mimic the way those influences actually affect behaviors in the organization, similar to the way a bubble chart works. Once understood, they can provide an additional tool for use in defining your plans to affect cultural change, and what to do to elevate the other functions toward parity. This is critical if you want all functions to perform to their potential.

Stakeholders is a word companies use to describe all of the people inside or outside the business who have a vested interest in its performance. To maximize the effectiveness of this definition, let's re-define it to include anyone on the inside or the outside of the business who can materially affect its "Response-Ability" to adapt and perform in its markets. Stakeholders on the outside of the organization can exert influence over the behaviors of those within it in ways that will impact decisions and even drive performance. Typically, it's through people who have business contact with those on the outside: the CEO, senior executives, sales personnel, a buyer, perhaps even the executive secretary.

To understand the dynamic a bit better, consider using spheres to represent factors that affect the ability of each organizational segment to make decisions and/or influence the activities of others, both inside and outside the organization. It's an important thing to understand when it comes to building your stakeholder list. The three primary spheres include: the social-organizational sphere, the customer sphere, and the regulatory sphere. The smaller spheres are used to represent the organization's individual functions and are positioned in the best place to represent where their own influences are coming from.

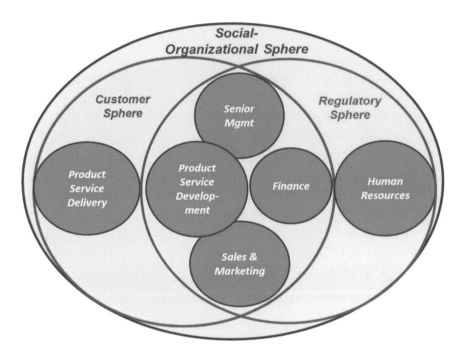

The Regulatory Sphere: In the day-to-day operation of many businesses, regulatory influences can often trump the others for their ability to impact decision making and process structure. Much of this is due to the weight of legal or compliance accountability that these requirements can impose, as well as the specific mandates that might be scripted within day-to-day operations. Regulations can influence every function from manufacturing, to transportation, to human resources and accounting. The actual existence, number, and importance of regulatory spheres will vary tremendously by industry. If you can imagine the difference between a pharmaceutical manufacturer, a government contractor, and a plumbing parts manufacturer, you might be able to guess at how much difference external regulations can impact each of them. One thing that's unique about regulatory spheres as compared to the others: compliance is much more absolute, which gives them the potential to be the strongest influencer of all.

    Customer Spheres: These spheres are second in the strength of influence because of the power exerted by the needs of your customers, and the "weighted by customer-centric" behaviors present in many types of organizations. Customer spheres can be surprisingly disruptive, because their requests can be less predictable and demanding, causing you to mobilize resources in response. The more "Response-Able" an organization is, the less disruptive these customer requests become.

Typically, customer requests will come into an organization either through the sales management teams or the executive offices, often causing "fire drills" of varying intensity. The size of your customer base also plays a large part in determining its influence, with smaller customer bases influencing more than broad ones. Even so, it isn't uncommon for them to alternate in strength with Social Spheres based on a specific business type or even at different times of the year.

Your Social Sphere: The influences that form the social sphere originate not only internally in the form of company specific (cultural) behaviors, but also externally from sources in the local community, or even sometimes more geo-political sources. One example of the latter might be social media, which has proven its ability to create rapid change (take note of the CEOs now making public apologies on social media). While this might be the least dominant group by virtue of their decentralized strengths, they can be more consistent in their behavior and as a result will impart policy influences, which have a tendency to be self-sustaining.

It's imperative to consider the impact spheres of influence can have on individual business functions when looking at how they are managed on a daily basis. An inordinate strength in one functional sphere (such as regulatory oversight in accounting) can often create an organizational weakness in the other functions if the regulatory responsibilities begin to over-reach their true requirements. Excessive approval and audit steps used to assert control can constrict process flow and dull response for delivery and services. Any function can suffer from an imbalance in influence: human resources, accounting and sales all have regulatory requirements to fulfill; human resources and the leadership team are heavily impacted by the local-social environment; and the operations and sales teams will be swayed by customer requirements and internal stakeholders. Maintaining mutually held, cross-functional objectives with disciplined timing for review and execution helps to balance task loads and deliverables, and the strategic management of timing (mile-markers of sorts) can be effective in neutralizing the negative effects of any influence.

As a member of the leadership team, your primary Response-Ability, is to assess and monitor the individual business functions and to help maintain a balance between the organization's needs and the individual influences that might drive them, thus preserving the best interests of the business from all aspects.

Motivating Response-Ably

Experience suggests there are numerous ways to motivate employees to perform admirably when faced with a deadline. One is the commonly used "burning platform," a metaphor designed to ignite engagement through a desire to avert disaster. Another might be the "Winning Team" approach, where the energy of success combined with a positive approach, is used to draw its participants into engaging, similar to that of a sports team. A last example might be referred to as the "benevolence" tactic, describing a change initiative that enlists engagement because it's for the mutual benefit of all stakeholders.

Which way is best? The answer really depends on a lot of things: the current performance of the business, the trajectory of its markets, the intensity of the competitive picture and the stability within the organization.

A burning platform can be effective in times of dire need: an unprofitable business, a declining customer base driven by poor performance, major/sudden changes in the market or the economy. However, this approach comes with both benefits and limitations. The immediacy of a burning platform can engender camaraderie of purpose within the organization and the imparted sense of urgency will rise to match the intensity of the "fire" rapidly galvanizing the team. The limitations are greater though: it must be a real condition, well-communicated and commonly understood by the organization credibly supported with actions and data. A false basis will undermine leadership credibility and ruin the effort. Further, any initiatives that arise must be focused on a specific set of results and when those results are met and the fire is extinguished, the activities must end, or be reset to a more normal timeline. Finally, the time frame for the initiative must be short, for just as a fire burning constantly alters in appearance and will die if not stoked, so the high energy stemming from an emergency will exhaust, as it is not perpetually sustainable.

Motivating a team under the guise of a winning theme can generate sufficient momentum to elevate the business to the next level, but not enough urgency to rescue it from a collapse. Business conditions that are viewed as generally acceptable might benefit from a winning change initiative, while a severely under-performing business would probably be a stretch, breeding doubt and disbelief in both the strategy as well as the competence of the leadership team.

The use of benevolence as a motivator bears merit, but lacks excitement. It draws its strength from the "what's in it for me" mindset, because of the mutual security that great improvement can generate. It can also at times be perceived as a diversion—absolving the individuals in the organization of the responsibility for the need to change under the guise of "someone else needs it." Improperly managed, benevolence commands less urgency, with a slower rate of commitment, and more relaxed buy-in than the others.

While a leader's individual style will play a strong factor in determining which motivational approach to use, the reality is that equal weight must be given to the current situation, including both the business condition and the organization's culture. More usefully, the motivations for all associates should be naturally engaged by the drivers for the initiative: failure means crisis management (burning platform), underachievement means turnaround management (winning team), modest success means transition to business excellence (mutual benefit) and more consistent success means market leadership or top-tier performance through business excellence (high-level mutual benefits). If the chosen motivational approach matches the business condition and its needs, associate buy-in becomes a natural function of its alignment with the confession of reality.

Work Enterprise-Wide

Working enterprise-wide involves demanding that each function in the business achieve balanced levels of high performance. Organizations will often develop specific excellence in narrow aspects of their business and exploit them to an acceptable level of overall success. By failing to strengthen the entirety of the organization to match the highest proficiency, they will nearly always underachieve to some degree. Exploiting a dominant organizational capability to success can result in a skewed business model that rises quickly on those strengths before falling under the weight of other under-performing elements when challenged by market changes, rapidly evolving conditions, or increases in scale, excessive focus on a sole strength may create unhealthy dependencies that can inhibit growth and under-achievement because of an inability to adapt. For example, a company that grows seismically by catering to the rapid success of one precious customer, compromising its performance with other customers while destabilizing other important company functions such as product design in the process, might experience a catastrophe with any change in that primary customer relationship.

One place to start developing an understanding is to identify the inter-relationships between each of the business functions. Look for connected responsibilities through project assignments and performance metrics, and seek to strengthen them. In doing so, you will begin to create a bond between them. The resultant synergies will improve collaboration and performance. Next, engage every single associate on each team by assigning them roles that support the objectives while also maintaining individual responsibility for the attainment of key metrics. Failing to fully close the loop with engagement could allow the individual processes to malfunction and end up eroding performance.

Consider a sales team that is calling all of the shots relative to its company's product offerings and the variety of features offered. Suppose further that the organization has fallen into the trap of offering nearly everything conceivable as options on the product, and, in the process, has impaired the ability of its operations team to deliver products to customers on time. Because every order had a customized appearance even when assembled from a group of standard offerings, the organization no longer regarded any of its products as standards, and it forced each of them through a customization step that added weeks to the completion time, without adding any real value. In our story, the customization process impeded their delivery response time by as much as 50%, costing them business.

In an effort to understand the above problem, we performed a classic analysis of the product options, their individual demand, and the revenue generation of each. We then teamed the accounting, manufacturing and engineering functions with the sales force and tasked them to cooperatively streamline offerings without losing business. The result was an impressive new line of standard product offerings with a focused set of custom options. In some cases, they were able to standardize certain options at no cost, gaining profitability from reduced internal processing, while in others we leveraged additional margin from specialized offerings. The solutions improved the fulfillment capability of the business while satisfying most critical customer requirements, and the improvement in market responsiveness actually increased sales in the very first year rather than losing market share due to any reduction in offerings.

Process Design

A company's processes are a critical evaluation point to begin facilitating an enterprise-wide transformation. When reviewing the designs for essential business processes, try to determine whether their input and the output deliverables flow through each appropriate function with the correct weighting and timing. Link your processing time to the market cadence to ensure a system response time that supports all of the other functions and ultimately the customer's requirements. The multi-functional deployment will help to avoid an overabundance of control or authority exerted by any single function. Carefully structured metrics and timing will support the creation of flow and drive decision-making that fulfills the organizations need to respond.

Let's look at an example of delivery to the customer, a key metric in nearly all businesses. If the delivery metric encompasses being on time to the customer's request, and the business sells a custom-engineered product, then achievement of an on-time metric must result from managing a sequence that moves through writing the order, engineering the solution, purchasing supply items and producing the product or service, all within the prescribed market expectations for timing. Too often, a failure to assign time limits causes the fulfillment process to break down and the customer expectation to be missed.

This timed connectivity works just like any type of sequenced activity. On a football field, the slower pulling guard is given a shorter distance to run to his blocking assignment or the faster running back will arrive ahead of his protection. In a manufacturing plant, parallel steps in the production sequence must be resource balanced to have nearly identical output capabilities. If they don't, the product doesn't flow smoothly, the effort is less productive and costs are elevated. And, in an office process such as payables, all of the steps in the payment process should be structured so that the payee is remunerated on time, every time, and so the process flows without a need for band aid approval steps. Referring back to the example in our story, if the response cycle time for engineering consumes too much of the system's order fulfillment time, the process steps must all be redesigned to be completed within the appropriate *Takt time*.

Maintaining enterprise-wide deployment ensures that not only will each department measure their processes using compatible metrics, but also that the processing steps and timing will be linked so as to provide a continuous flow of activity that is consistent with the demands in its markets. Extending the story example further, if the processing through engineering is four weeks, procurement another four weeks, and manufacturing is 18 weeks—accumulating to a total completion time of 26 weeks—in a market that will only tolerate 16 weeks, there is a clear disconnect to resolve. By starting at the customer and translating the market requirements back through the company's processes, they can be reengineered to that baseline, or at least a better one. Once achieved, your ability to consistently hit your commitments for customer or market response will improve.

The last component of working enterprise-wide is organizational focus, and this involves aligning the entire organization's priorities around achievement of the key business objectives.

Creating organizational focus is one of the most difficult aspects of transformational change because of the constant need to maintain your leadership team's engagement in initiatives across all functional lines. It's within the individual functional silos where activities and priorities can become de-coupled from the primary goals, diminishing your ability to achieve key initiatives. These activities have to be carefully managed to support functional excellence while at the same time ensuring cross-functional involvement on the key initiatives. Keeping the key initiatives, the high-level metrics, and the related local timing requirements in front of people will facilitate consistent prioritization and alignment to the right functional objectives.

Prioritization can be easily clarified by *triangulating* your initiative objectives among the customer's critical needs, those of the business and the market requirements. These three points will ground them to reality, while addressing the real challenges in the business. Further, they will also lend credibility to the vision, which in turn helps associates to commit themselves to a more clearly identified change initiative. The factual basis for your priorities enables the alignment of everyone's implementation tasks into a focused plan that achieves the desired result. Any activities tied to non-critical initiatives should then be placed on hold or ceased completely to avoid wasted resources and allow for focused effort.

Once you've narrowed the initiatives list to a manageable size and the teams are assigned, it's time to perform a group evaluation to understand the initiatives' impact to the overall culture. Looking at the teams, you should quantify the individual strengths, weaknesses and technical and interpersonal skills present each. Your goal is to unearth two types of associates: 1) those who might inhibit implementation due to lack of either skills or willingness and 2) those who will facilitate it. This evaluation will identify opportunities for redeployment in order to balance team memberships with appropriate skills, and where to position the strongest leaders in order to leverage your success on the key initiatives.

Strengthening and aligning the organizations cross-functional relationships also helps accelerate decision making. With the vision established, the achievement plan outlined and the definition of cross-functional teams underway, the task assignments should be distributed as evenly as possible throughout the organization. The old adage of "work gravitating to those who get the job done" must be avoided through active management of the deployment. Individual associate evaluations will assist you in balancing the player strength on each team, e.g. an associate who might potentially inhibit progress can be neutralized by positioning a stronger person who is capable of managing for success. Finally, it's important to break down the vision level metrics into more granular local measures (team or functional level) that are aligned to specific projects. Properly identified, these should feed the vision level metrics.

Focus becomes even more sustainable when the plan accounts for the long-term involvement required by all associates. Your enterprise-wide approach will support a more balanced set of business objectives that enables steady improvement and promotes sustainment. It's this balance that minimizes excessive influence by any single business function. In essence, the overall group focus is migrated all the way down to the individual associates through assigned actions and group related personal objectives. We touched on this in chapter one with the sequenced need for understanding the organization, translating the vision into actions, and deploying those actions across the organization, in the process, balancing the level of change across all segments of the team.

Response-Able Planning and Execution Are the Keys to Success.

A business leader's style must reflect their organization's values, ethics and mission. As we advocated in this chapter, leaders must also practice their responsibilities with the same disciplined sense of timing required by the competitive markets they participate in. Reinforced by the leadership, this timing can have a transformational influence on organizational performance.

"Good business leaders create a vision, articulate the vision, passionately own the vision, and relentlessly drive it to completion." Jack Welch

Over my career I've learned that small plans breed small results, and allow for contentment in underachievement. Since I'm a firm believer that more than 95% of your employees *want* to do a *great* job, you can embrace your leadership role by positioning them to be fully prepared to tackle the opportunities and challenges that lie ahead of them. How effective you are at motivating them and sustaining their desire will define your success. Making your vision "visual" to the stakeholders who depend on your business is *your* leadership Response-Ability.

Chapter 3: RADical Simplification

Using the Success Equation: Results = Approach + Deployment

1. "Root" your vision with targeted Results

2. Plan your "Approach"

3. Deploy to engage and inform

4. Use Results to "Course Correct" your way to continuous improvement

"Now, let's take a moment to talk about the Malcolm Baldrige Performance Excellence Award." Even the eyes that weren't on me looked up and the stunned silence in the room bordered on disbelief. "Not because we should apply for it, but because the application process for that award would ask us to look at the processes we use to run our business in a very simple way. It's been useful in helping me focus on success through many different initiatives. The prior version of the Baldrige assessment divided the key processes of a business into seven areas and then looked at the processes used in each of those areas to ensure that the *approach,* or the way they are built, takes into consideration and also fulfills the needs of all of the stakeholders in the business. By stakeholders they mean owners, associates and even customers—anyone with a vested interest. Next, it asks the business to ensure that our process *deployment* broadly engages all of those stakeholders whose involvement would contribute to the successful operation of the process. Finally, they ask applicants to define the expected *results* of using that process in a way that fulfills all of the objectives of the business. The more current version of the process has replaced the results question by asking the applicant to evaluate their key approaches for Leanings that can improve performance, and then how their approaches align with current and future organizational needs.

"For now, however, I'm going to stick with results and actually begin in reverse. It's been my experience that the actual set of target results is often predetermined by market benchmarks, corporate mandates, demands from customers or even competitive market pressures. Because of this, it makes sense to consider our desired results first, and then determine an approach and a deployment plan that will enable us to achieve them. Re-stated in the modified order, we begin with a grounded, targeted objective (result) that satisfies needs of all potential stakeholders. We'll then need to figure out how to approach that objective to make it more achievable before deciding who to involve (deployment) to ensure our success. I call this my 'Success Formula: R=A+D.' Now, having said all of that, starting with the first Baldrige process, Leadership, would anyone like to try to identify some of the sources of our targeted results? If we have a Leadership process, what results should we expect from it?"

"What leadership processes do we have?" asked an accounting manager.

"I would think business planning could be called a process," Maria suggested.

"What about strategy? Isn't that a leadership process?" Geoff asked.

"Actually, strategy is a category all its own," I answered.

"Well, what about budgeting and staffing?" Maria asked.

"Certainly, both of those are the responsibility of leadership at some point in time," I said. "But let's take another angle. Can anyone other than Maria give me an example of a human resources process?"

"How about performance appraisals!" blurted one of the engineering leaders.

"Do we do any employee development? If so, that could be one," Sarah, the accounting manager, interjected.

"Thanks a lot!" Maria smiled as she said it. "At least I now have someone to target for this year's appraisal training and development!"

"That will get you a *targeted result,*" joked a member of the operations team.

Amused, I stepped into the banter, "Okay, we're getting some traction now. Someone please take a shot at the list of stakeholders for an employee development process."

"Wouldn't it be the employees and their supervisors?" Dick offered.

"Are there any others?" I prodded.

"How about the company's customers and owners?" Maria offered.

"How so?"

"Well, if the performance appraisal process delivers improved performance, don't both the customer and the company owners win?"

"Good point. We probably should consider the ways owners and customers might benefit from the process. I'm not sure about including them in the deployment group, though."

I turned on a screen to display the seven categories, along with a short checklist under each. In order, they included Leadership, Strategy, Customer Focus, Information Management, Human Resources, Process Management and Results.

"Using the definitions on this list as a basis, I'd like all of you to break into two groups and quickly arrange all of our existing processes under the most appropriate category. When we come back together, we can compare the two lists and iron out any differences of opinion."

The teams broke, moving to opposite sides of the room. The entire exercise took less than an hour, and when we came back together, it wasn't surprising to see that not only were some of the categorizations different, but each list contained processes that the other didn't. It seemed to be confirmation that there were both formal and informal processes at work in the business, something that would need to be changed.

The conversation around adjusting the categorizations went fairly quickly and without any contention. A few of the perceived informal processes were deemed to be sub-processes of a main one, and a couple of others made their way onto a "to be formalized" list.

The teams dug in and worked hard to select their project lists, assign objectives and develop a deployment plan that would engage the entire organization. With my continued reminders to keep the plan simple, rooted and deployable, they did a good job pulling together a first draft.

"Now that we've identified and categorized your business initiatives, I'd like to return to square one and recheck each process using R=A+D," I said.

Again, what result do we expect from each initiative? Do the actions appear to support its achievement? And finally, how complete does our deployment plan look from a functional perspective?

Judging by the silence hanging in the room, they certainly hadn't seen that one coming. After a few moments an engineering leader asked, "Uh…how, exactly, are we supposed to do that?"

"Before we proceed on building our strategy deployment matrix, we'll need to take a couple of steps back and confirm that we have a clear understanding that each initiative makes sense 'directionally' for the business by how it supports the results targets," I explained. "It's just a quick back-check and isn't intended to second guess what we've already done. We can then assemble them into a draft approach to achieve the results targets, based on what we know now. Finally, we can build the deployment teams based on the affected areas." I smiled and added, "I know it sounds complicated, but for now we'll keep it as simple as possible and avoid excessive detail."

A few people tapped away on their tablets.

"Try to maintain the point of view of the audience listening to us when it comes time to deploy to individual teams. If we can't explain them with both clarity and an appearance of attainability, their buy-in will be suspect," I added

"But some of these goals look impossible." The entire engineering team nodded in agreement with this comment.

"It's okay if results targets are difficult, but we do have to be sure they are achievable. If they don't appear attainable, people won't even engage. If they look too easy, then they won't impact our current behaviors enough to generate cultural change. We have to give them credible attainment plans, and keep them rooted to the facts that support our vision as it was developed earlier, in order to keep it a reality instead of a hallucination. That's what this entire process will do for us so long as we do the work correctly."

The metrics review only took about an hour because they felt the factual criteria that had influenced their choice of targeted results were difficult to argue with. Certainly, some of the goals appeared to stretch beyond what this team felt it was capable of. Nevertheless, I encouraged them to leave the goals as-is for the time being to see if they could build approach plans with milestones that would make them appear more attainable, grounding them closer to reality. Once again, they split into teams and worked through the same methods of refining the approach they would use. Next, they revisited the project list for its ability both to achieve the results and satisfy all of the stakeholder needs.

Finally, we tackled deployment in a similar fashion, confirming who needed to be included and defining the level of involvement, from leadership roles to "hands-in" activities. We re-examined our approach options to better focus on maintaining broad involvement through the rollout to build engagement and buy-in. Each group was asked to establish follow-up procedures that would enable timely intervention as needed to remain on track, and also to define the points at which we would celebrate success.

"As we put the final touches on our strategy deployment matrix, we'll need to keep thinking about how to translate these plans into the words and thoughts of the people we'll be presenting them to. This step is critical for us to insure group buy-in. Our explanations should clearly make a connection to how we have rooted stretch objectives to the needs of the business and its associates. It's the only way to build credibility within the entire organization."

Give your vision "roots" with targeted Results

As we said earlier in chapter 1, deriving the objectives for your vision from the needs of both your external and internal customers, market benchmarks, and other tangible sources creates objectives that have "roots," aiding in your associates' ability to understand and trust them. These needs present themselves in the form of desired "Results," such as delivery and quality performance, product and services offerings, financial performance and even regulatory demands. Translating them into an objective set requires navigating between those targets that are clearly possible and others that appear transformational.

That isn't to say that you should shy away from something that looks impossible from the perspective of your current performance. If there is market-driven evidence to demonstrate that a given objective target *is* possible (one example might be Amazon Prime's 2-day shipping), then all you need to be realistic about is the timeline you'll decide upon to implement it in. The same principle applies for unprecedented goals, back to the John Kennedy example of putting a man on the moon. Because it was an extension of existing technology, no matter how fledgling that technology appeared, the lengthy timeline still made it appear possible.

Not all of your visionary objectives have to be rooted, but most of them should be. Too many unproven targets will cloud the appearance of attainability and can create dissent amongst your associates.

Although results may not always seem like the most logical starting point to frame an initiative, the pressure exerted from influences such as competition, customer requirements, regulatory impacts, technological advances, shareholder expectations, financial pressure from lending institutions, and internal employee needs will impose many objective targets for you. These targets should link to and drive your business strategy, directly creating some initiatives and demanding a response that can also serve as a call to action. These external examples will also help ensure that your objectives aren't constrained by internalized thinking, allowing them to function as the roots of your vision. In many cases an urgently needed response can singlehandedly "root" a stretch objective, creating a mandate for its attainment.

Targeted results can also help to identify reasonable expectations for an effort. What kind of return on investment can be expected for the business in the form of process improvements? How can you ensure that those results will support the fulfillment of the vision, and how can they be sustained? The origin and immediacy of any result requirement will help to define how you should go about delivering it.

This chapter was titled R=A+D to identify the power that external and internal drivers can (and should) have to predetermine a set of required results and their influence on how you approach the problem. Without this, your objectives might be defined solely by internal pressures and traditional thinking and limited by the perception of the ability to improve over your current state. Managing a business to internally derived objectives is a pitfall that can result in substandard performance at the customer that is unaddressed, causing failure. A former boss of mine used to refer to this as "drinking your own bathwater," more correctly explained as managing your metrics to deliver the answers you were looking for. You have to honestly believe that basing your objective set primarily on the needs of the market, the owners, customers, and employees is the right thing to do, and that the needs of the business will be satisfied through the correct strategy. Otherwise, if your objective targets become too internalized, your "drink of the day" could be a bathwater cocktail.

Using the appropriate external and internal information to develop target metrics will frame the vision, and your final metrics can be dialed into based on what's needed, wanted, or possible (I say "possible" very carefully). This maintains a set of results that 1) satisfies the needs of stakeholders, 2) is meaningful, 3) can be clearly communicated, and 4) is broadly deployable. Excessive metrics will dilute focus, so maintaining an essential set of key metrics that are clearly defined keeps them more readily attainable. To guarantee a simple and effective, but thorough impact on the organization, focus your metrics on five traditional areas, plus a sixth – less traditional factor. By priority, the general categories I typically use and recommend for manufacturing are:

1. **Safety (or) Wellness: Employees First.** While manufacturing and construction companies are often "Safety First," other companies should consider putting employee well-being up front.

2. **Quality: Customer Focused.** External customer "touching" first, with a second level that is internal-process focused.

3. **Delivery: Customer Focused.** Delivery of products and/or services that meet customer needs within or better than the market defined expectations.

4. **Cost: External (Market) Focused.** The total cost of delivered products or services to the customer, measured against any available competitive benchmarks.

5. **Cost: Internal Focused.** A key metric for cost of operating performance

6. **Time:** A business response metric that is market defined and can be adjusted and deployed in some form to the entire enterprise.

We'll examine different aspects of this results list further in chapter eight, and dive more deeply into how to prioritize and manage them. For now, I'll just stress that it's equally critical to insure each result is measured in a meaningful and accurate way that is representative of how the customer of that metric wants to see it. This helps you to keep all of your metrics clearly defined, easy to understand, and targeted on achievements that will transform the performance of your business. Consistency and accuracy in measurement are a key element for getting people to trust and gain confidence in your goals.

Plan your Approach

Once your targeted results have been agreed upon, it's time to define the initiatives you'll need to achieve them, also called your **Approach**. Although the targets themselves may in part dictate the way you tackle them, the information gathered while triangulating from past performance, competitor positions, and customer needs can also help to shape the list of possible actions. Your choice of attainment projects must be comprehensive enough to bridge the gap from your current level of performance to that of the new target. If you continually evaluate your position between your current state and the respective targets, you'll need to challenge your employees to adjust their own tactical plans in support of objective attainment. This empowerment also helps build credibility further through the way that it supports the broader interests of all stakeholders.

As a leader, the pressure for day-to-day results can make it difficult to focus on all of the various complexities during the launch of a change initiative. These pressures can come from an urgent customer request, a corporate mandate, or even investors placing short-term profit demands. It isn't unusual to see veteran leaders jump ahead and formulate objectives based upon the need to respond without considering how to implement them or even to understand the greater impact on the business. Your approach to the daily management of strategic initiatives must take that into consideration, maintaining consistent follow-up, while leaving room for diversions. Start your reviews at a high level and allow them to expand in detail as they deploy to the rest of the organization. All large-scale change initiatives blossom into greater detail at each phase of implementation planning, but that level of detail is too complex when viewed from top to bottom and it can't be effectively managed in its entirety by one individual. Arranging for the detail management to be conducted at the appropriate organizational or functional level ensures that it's deployed in a way that keeps it manageable and helps to maintain continuity.

Supporting the implementation plan with reporting disciplines that focuses everyone on the results at their own levels keeps things simple. The lower level details will develop into assignments for those folks at the working level. By performing status reviews at the functional level plus one-level-up for normal performance, they remain concise and allow for efficient problem escalation when issues arise. When performance is in doubt, you should expand your review oversight to two-levels to increase the speed of decision making and expand the options for corrective action. This eliminates the need for managers to maintain detailed knowledge of all programs and helps associates zero in on the corrective actions required. At the leadership level, you'll maintain a triple view of the objectives, one focused on the performance of the vision level (global) metrics, another at activities taking place at the highest initiative level, and a third view of the metrics that are off track at any level. Everything below these are reviewed between each working group and two levels of managers, but only the global metrics are reviewed publicly. Driving out the multiple levels of detail helps to keep the vision's initiatives easily understandable, improving engagement and improving their sustainability.

In staying true to the goal of keeping it simple to make it sustainable, your leadership task is to facilitate a basic level of organization-wide understanding of the top-level metrics and how they deploy downward. Simplifying this information supports everyone's ability to engage in the planning and communication activities that satisfy both functional and personal needs. It will also enable each individual to understand how their assignments contribute to attainment of the vision.

Deploy to engage and inform

Building engagement in the implementation of your strategy is greatly aided by directly recruiting the involvement of the associates who are integral to achieving the improvements—those who utilize and refine processes, and the ones who will mutually benefit from the effort. Once you've assessed the skills and resources necessary for the success of each strategic project, a more balanced deployment plan will involve a cross-section of all of the potential stakeholders and can increase your chances of success.

Encourage your associates to fill in the details of your organizational initiatives by asking each respective team to view the importance of their initiative from the perspective of all affected stakeholders. You'll need their assistance in defining the specific projects needed to achieve those objectives. They will also help to uncover any necessary information, establish the lower level metrics, and possibly even identify the need for external resources. A thorough approach in the deployment stage should satisfy the resource requirements for each project by assigning teams that are balanced in size relative to priority.

Deployment efforts should have three key objectives; 1) focused protection of stakeholder interests, 2) contribution to initiative success, and 3) broad involvement of the organization. Engagement on the project teams and in task-related personal goals helps connect associates directly to the initiatives and gives them a stake in the outcome. This participation further helps associates to understand how their individual goal performance drives projects and how these contributions accumulate to successfully achieving the planned strategy. Hands-on involvement in uncovering the "roots" helps to link the "stretch" for any goal closer to reality. In many cases, this deployment can often be extended to anyone touched by the initiative; in others, the size of the group can be reduced to only those required for implementation. In certain cases, involvement could even be extended outward to customers and other stakeholders. No matter the technique used to involve them, broadly engaging everyone who will play a significant role in the implementation or sustainment of the specific goal enhances your odds of success.

A correctly structured deployment plan has two components. First, it requires a finalized project list with all non-priority projects cast aside. Second, both of the afore-mentioned structure and staffing evaluations should be completed so that all limitations in skills and resources become known and adjusted for. The deliverables—a clean task list, skills gaps resolved, balanced resources assigned to each project, and strategic placement of developing leadership—are the requisites for good deployment.

Strengthen your deployment effort from the beginning by assigning project leadership roles to the best and the brightest in the organization—those employees with either natural or experiential leadership skills. Since all team structures should be cross-functional, the functional origin of the potential leaders isn't always critical, unless the project requires specific technical skills or regulatory knowledge. In making your assignments, don't allow technical skills to trump leadership skills, as the latter are far more important. Each functional leader should be assigned a mentor—one best fulfilled by the senior staff champion for the top-level initiative.

Once these leadership roles are established, each team should be equipped with the proper technical skills, allocated through the cross functional assignments. Use the staffing evaluation to balance the strength of the players. As an example, it's wise to counter a potentially problematic associate with another that is oppositely strong. Though there are many reasons for retaining a "problem-child" on a given team—usually because of critical experience or key technical expertise—the presence of too many "difficult" associates might indicate the need for a different kind of project structure.

When planning your deployment, observe some basic rules. Try to avoid excessive multiple team assignments—important especially for the leaders. If a leader has been rated as developmental, bolster them with a good mentor, a good development plan, and a stronger team. If there are new employees, make sure to place them in a group where their leader and the associates assigned with them can help them to acclimate and flourish rather than being excluded due to a lack of internal knowledge. Sticking to these rules will absolutely yield both a better change initiative, a better result and an organization that grows.

Use Results as a guide to course correct your way to continuous improvement

Establishing your results targets up front or, taking aim at the "R," will support the development of objectives that align with all of your external and internal customers as well as your business strategy. They also serve to establish a sound basis for those goals that will hold up under public scrutiny.

Nearly every change initiative will have results targets that are either too aggressive or too conservative. Using your results monitoring process to continually refine these targets is necessary to ensure that performance is optimized. We said earlier that the monitoring of all sub-level measures would be done either in a level-up format, or through exception management. It's the exception management part of the process that should initiate a multi-level review for both steering corrective actions or goal adjustments.

It's difficult to say when an adjustment should be made, but I would recommend considering one any time a metric is trending to be either missed or significantly exceeded. When corrective actions cannot rescue a metric, or when it is trending so far above the target that is it certain to be exceeded, it might be time to extrapolate the trending result and develop new objectives that improve over that trend, resetting the goal. The biggest reason for doing this is to avoid motivational problems that will reduce the effort level—being convinced of failure or on the converse, assured of an easy success.

Summary

The Results / Approach / Deployment methodology is a sound way to ensure that the criteria used to define your business objectives will "root" solidly to the overall business needs. Careful planning and thorough engagement are required to ensure that your initiatives list is sufficiently fleshed out to support those objective targets. At that same time a deployment plan that enables broad involvement in both project implementation and measurement of success will build engagement through execution and meet the fundamental needs for success in any change initiative.

With all of R=A+D identified, your results can be monitored and adjustments made to stay on track, and you will have the option to revise objective targets up or down based on the progress achieved.

For all three phases—Results, Approach, and Deployment—a feedback and improvement cycle is useful to facilitate consistent and predictable improvements. The active monitoring and adjustment part of the process is what the "R" is all about, and with the addition of timely follow up, misses to the target can be avoided entirely, or corrected and made up before they accumulate into a loss.

So, how do results, approach, and deployment build disciplines and simplify the process? Because consistent and timely monitoring of progress and diligence in asking the same series of questions for each action will keep a clearer focus on the objectives and the path to success. The simplicity of this successful equation is an enabler for an organization to target, involve, and reward key stakeholders, providing a simpler way to "back-check" and avoid confusion. By using the "Success Equation" to confirm that each objective has passed through the logical sequence of targeting Results, defining the Approach, and using them to build the Deployment plan, you will maintain the clarity of your objectives in the eyes of those tasked with their implementation. Prepare your communication plans carefully (to avoid unwanted surprises and negative perception as the initiative is rolled out) and quickly advertise your achievements to accelerate the plans credibility.

The deployment step in the process also provides a sustainable method of ensuring organizational engagement, breaking the top-level objectives down into tasks while maintaining linkage throughout the organization. It creates a direct connection between each employee's individual goals and their daily work, a critical step that's often poorly executed. Be wary of deployment that's too thin or insufficiently cross-functional—these issues can break the process down and cause under-achievement. The organization-wide participation must be comprehensive, and the engagement must be continually monitored.

Chapter 4 will look at how to prepare your organization for change, both physically and mentally. Keep in mind the words of Lisa Bodell as we progress:

"Change cannot be put on people. The best way to instill change is to do it with them. Create it with them."

Chapter 4: Organizational Change

Launch Your Strategy with High-Performance Staffing

1. **Isaac Newton's Laws of … Change?**

2. **Preparing for Change**

3. **Building Engagement**

4. **Measure Impact!**

As the framework of our change initiative began to take shape, it became clear to us that the projects we had identified would demand resource requirements that exceeded those of the existing organization. In order to resolve the problem, we scheduled a session to assess the readiness of the organization's resources to adopt and implement the strategy. Having taken a two-week break following completion of our strategic initiatives, the team reconvened to an offsite location so that we could better assess the overall organization and develop a plan to close those resource gaps.

I explained our task to the group, "So now that we've put some definition to our overall strategy and have identified the initiatives and projects that will enable us to achieve it, we need to look at our organization and our people from two perspectives. First, we're going to look at the skills present in the organization to see if we have everything needed to implement our new strategy. We'll also assess where those skill-sets are placed to be sure they are in the right places. This is called "Structure." Next, we'll look at the depth of our organization's resources to confirm that our available capacity is correctly allocated for us to move forward. This step is called Staffing.

We started with a brief review of the strategy and the draft list of projects to serve as something of a reminder. Our purpose was to focus on those initiatives that might require special capabilities and expose any gaps in our existing skillsets. In preparation, every staff member was asked to assemble a functionally-based skills inventory for their teams, identifying any needs that weren't covered. When combined into an assessment of the entire organization, it would provide a template for us to compare to the one we had previously identified in our strategic sessions.

With the skills inventory matched to our needs, we next started looking for options to fill the gaps internally with people who either possessed the skills or with ones who had demonstrated enough developmental potential to acquire them in the timeframe allowed by the strategy. In some cases, it became a negotiation, as one staff member would try to coerce another out of a key team member.

"I need an engineering technical specialist for our product development team to help us develop new controls packages. It's a highly cost-effective approach to provide high margin options," John said, offering the first need.

"There is a young tech in our maintenance department who is a complete whiz at the controls systems on our machines," Geoff replied. "His name is Bob Patel and though I would hate to lose him, I really think you should take a hard look at him before we start to search outside."

"In that event, we'll need to recruit anyway, if for nothing else than to replace him on the maintenance team," Maria said. "Thanks for offering, Geoff, it's great team play!"

"The Marketing team could use someone like an internet marketing specialist," Dick said. "We're finding that we aren't doing nearly as much online as our competitors, and this shoe leather marketing we currently do is slow and expensive."

"Great job to both of you!" I commented. "The specialized skills inherent to those positions could be pivotal to our strategy and if we can't fill them from within quickly enough, we'll have to go outside. They need to be filled before progress can be made in those areas." We finished this step by prioritizing a plan to close each of the gaps.

With the gap analysis session completed, the next task was to estimate whether the organization possessed enough overall resource capacity to tackle the entire list of business-critical initiatives and projects. During the strategy sessions, we had taken the implementation plan down to the project level so that we could make some "directional estimates" of the resources required. Understanding that precision was nearly impossible, we left provisions to abandon certain lower priority projects or to involve outside resources where the payoff merited. The final resource estimates would be confirmed by the project teams after they kicked off their initial group reviews.

"Well, the first part was easy. If you need a rocket scientist to build a rocket and you don't have one, it's obvious you'll need to go out and hire one. It's either that or you don't build the rocket."

"Now let's talk about resource capacity."

"Certainly, we need more resources than we can afford in order to keep the pace we've identified in our plans," Maria observed. "So, now we know that the million-dollar question is: Who's going to volunteer to take on that task? What do we change in order to acquire resources we aren't budgeted to pay for?"

I smiled grimly and nodded my understanding. "Belt tightening is never easy. It's going to come down to a matter of priorities. If we agree that a certain resource is vital for the fiscal recovery of our overall operation, we'll have to obtain that resource even if it means having to reduce somewhere else.

"This is triage, folks. We can't worry about bruises, scrapes, and cuts when there are puncture wounds elsewhere. Make no mistake about it, we're bleeding profusely in certain aspects of our business, and if we don't stem the losses in those areas, the whole body will die." I gave that a moment to sink in before continuing, "Okay, Dick, since cash flow is the lifeblood of any business, let's hear from you first about our company's sales potential."

Dick stayed seated, shuffled some papers, cleared his throat and began. "Well, from the perspective of pure capacity, we desperately need a second sales manager for the West Coast. Our competitors are killing us out there. There's plenty of business to be gained, but we just don't have the personnel out there to capitalize on all the opportunities."

"Do we have good distribution there?" I asked.

"We've got a presence," Dick said flatly, "but it isn't great and that's part of the problem."

"Is the market size adequate?" Although I'd had some forewarning of his response, my leading question was more for the benefit of the team. "How does the market size and revenue generation potential compare to some of our higher-performing territories?"

"Let's not talk apples versus oranges," said Dick. "West Coast doesn't compare to the other territories because they buy at an entirely different end of the market. However, our range of products includes many we could be selling out there—things those businesses need and have the capital to purchase. The problem is, as I said before, we have no one out there knocking on doors and writing up orders. We've been missing out on this growth potential for years. It's as if we've sent one person out there with a tablespoon and asked him to divert the waterfall."

"You sound pretty certain of yourself," I said.

"It's all basic research," said Dick. He slid a document across the table to me. "Here's the report I filed six months ago to your predecessor. It verifies the market size, the contracted distribution, and the phenomenal potential for upside growth. I've said all along that an initial investment in the West Coast will pay off handsomely. My pleas have fallen on deaf ears."

I examined the paper. He'd done his homework; the numbers looked impressive.

"This is an example of the kind of breakthrough action we need to help us hit our objectives," I said. "Okay, Dick, we're listening to you now. We'll add this proposal to the draft plan. I'll have our folks in Accounting confirm your projections, and then we'll take final action."

I could see by Dick's facial expression that he was equal parts surprised and pleased. Others around the table also responded pleasantly. It was becoming clear to me that this leadership team already had some good strategies for turning things around, and for one reason or another, they hadn't been implemented. They were going to appreciate being taken seriously for a change.

The structure and capacity deliverables were necessary for us to assess the team's physical capability to deliver the strategy. Through the course of the discussion, we were able to identify nearly all of the skills gaps, and we gained a rough understanding of the areas where resource adjustments or program timing would need to be reevaluated in order to match our human capacity to demand.

The last step in the process was to discuss areas where our functional structure might not allow for appropriate focus or be able to support the momentum requirements of the strategy.

"All right," I said, "let's now see if we can identify any areas that aren't in position to support the speed of project implementation."

"I know that my HR team will have difficulty with all of this," Mary stated. "The corporation is rolling out a new corporate benefits program that will take a lot of our effort in the fourth quarter. The follow-up requirements for the results of our employee survey get more stringent every year, and we've got that new mandatory safety program as well. Diverting key members of my team to support these new initiatives, even cross-functionally, is going to be a problem."

"My accounting team is already buried!" Jolene chimed in. "There are new financial sub-systems being implemented, and we're targeted to reduce the process time for monthly closing by yet another day. I just don't know how to get it done!"

"But that sounds like your whole team will free up a day," I said teasingly. She looked back, clearly unamused.

Dick added, "Our customer service people aren't equipped to deal with the number of customer 'touches' we currently have. If you also want them to chase down forecasting information at the same time, they need to follow up on order satisfaction, they're going to be spread too thin. It just won't happen."

I shook my head in disagreement. "You aren't grasping the bigger picture. Keep in mind that some of the initiatives we've identified will reduce or even eliminate many of the rework-type activities that are currently chewing up your teams' day. Our processes also need to be streamlined. I'm asking you to 'spend ahead' a bit and commit. The cross-functional team structure will help maintain program momentum when any one group like accounting gets bogged down. If necessary, we'll adjust our expectations sensibly according to the rate of progress and hold weekly barrier meetings to keep obstructions from slowing us down."

I knew from experience that these team structure and process issues were relatively easy to spot from the inside. Using a nominal amount of process data—including snapshots of the receivables and payables cycles, purchase order approval timing, and other performance information for some of the key processes—we were able to identify some early trouble spots in customer service and accounting. From there we put together a containment plan that could quickly mitigate them with some resource re-allocation and/or reporting changes.

The end product of this structure session included a shopping list for the specific skillsets and a reorganization plan that would optimize our ability to achieve the strategy. A couple of weeks later, we held a second offsite session to conduct the staffing assessments and to identify leadership candidates, high-potential associates, and those team members who presented performance concerns. By spreading these two sessions over a couple of weeks it gave the leadership team time to both recover from the first session as well as prepare for the second one. This time we simply conducted a 360-degree roundtable to discuss each functional organization. The senior manager described each individual's performance history, followed by a group commentary.

"Now let's start our performance discussions with HR. Who better to set an example on how to assess and manage performance than the people who help develop our evaluation standards?" I almost made Maria wince with that one, but she took the challenge.

"I'll start with Gwen, my HR Labor Manager. From my view, she is bright, articulate, driven, and responsive. The quality of her work is excellent, and she has no issues regarding attendance or personal problems. In other words, I would rate her promotable into my position within a year." Maria paused, indicating it was up to me to finish this report.

"Would anyone like to comment on Gwen?" I asked. There were no immediate takers. "Okay, then, based on my own early interactions with her, I would tend to agree that she is someone with genuine leadership potential. Anything I've asked of her has been completed promptly and correctly."

Geoff cleared his throat. "Maybe that's why I can't get anything out of her," he said. "Whenever I ask her for something, there is always a reason I can't get it. Plus, she is often rude to my supervisors."

"I would agree with that," Janet added. "It doesn't matter what I ask her for, I just don't get it."
Maria wasn't happy. "I guess it would have been nice to know this earlier."

"Maybe we've just been focused on getting her to change one on one," Dick said apologetically.

"Okay, let's keep things going by doing this. Maria will talk to each of you and give Gwen some feedback based on her performance with her internal customers. I'll let Maria decide if the problems are serious enough to work a formal development plan into her performance evaluation, or if an informal improvement plan will do the trick."

We continued through each staff member in a similar manner, limiting the time we spent so that we could finish in a single day. Once again, the objectives were to identify leadership development candidates, balance resource assignments to the strategy teams, and provide an action plan to address anyone needing a development or improvement plan. When we completed the staffing review, we returned to the structural gap analysis one final time to confirm whether the higher-performing internal candidates we earmarked could be reassigned to fill the key skills and capacity gaps or whether it would be necessary for us to recruit from outside the company.

In the ensuing weeks, we began to implement the identified organizational adjustments. To minimize nervousness, we started with the all of the positive moves, publicizing them broadly to encourage everyone to engage in them. Next, we held individual sessions with the associates rated as competent, to reassure them of their continuing roles. Finally, we tackled improvement plans for those associates with developmental or performance concerns, handling them behind the scenes and tasking them individually to improve their level of contribution. As we moved forward, it was clear that our approach, communication, investment in preparation, and broad involvement in developing the initiative plans, metrics, and teams was paying off with greater employee involvement. The organization seemed more at ease with the changes, giving us a positive start.

While participating in a senior leadership development program for a major industrial company, I was invited into a group discussion on culture with the company's CEO. During the course of that discussion, he made a statement that has never left me: "Culture is more powerful than strategy. When culture goes up against strategy, it wins ten out of ten times." Now I'm sure one interpretation or another of that statement has found its way into management books countless times over the years, and I'm equally certain that I'd heard a different version or two of it before, but perhaps because his recital came at a time when I was in the midst of leading my own major change initiative, it resonated tremendously. Why? Because changes in strategy are *never* independent of the need for some level of cultural change! The executive challenge is to set into motion those changes that improve upon an organization's weaknesses while at the same time preserving its strengths. A quote by Frances Hesselbein supports this:

"Culture does not change because we desire to change it. Culture changes when the organization is transformed; the culture reflects the realities of people working together every day."

Although I would always refer to any cultural change process as an evolutionary one, it isn't meant to imply that radical change isn't necessary. In truth, it's sometimes unavoidable. Some types of rapidly infused changes—reorganizations, product line or facility rationalizations, and other abrupt moves that might be required for survival, can also be effective at energizing the "inertia wheel" of change. I believe Sir Isaac Newton's famous "Laws" can be used to describe the physics of cultural change.

Newton's Laws . . . of Change?

A truly "strategic" initiative will require some type of motivational "inertia" to stimulate its culture to engage in the changes. To help explain how this works in application, I'll use all three of Newton's laws of motion, starting with his first, the law of inertia. To implement a strategy in a culture that's essentially "at rest," the first half of his law applies:

"An object at rest will remain at rest unless acted on by an unbalanced force."

Getting your change initiative rolling requires a level of effort greater than the size of the mass (the organization and/or its market) to get the "inertia wheel" turning. In this case, the "unbalanced force" becomes the application of an energy that is contained within the strategy and amplified by the speed and breadth of its deployment. Both are required to energize the organization into motion.

Now, think of the organization and its market(s) as the equivalent of Newton's "mass." His second law states:

"Acceleration is produced when a force acts on a mass. The greater the mass [of the object being accelerated] the greater the amount of force needed [to accelerate it]."

The more extensive your strategy, the more of your organization you'll have to engage to supply momentum; in other words, the greater the mass, the greater the energy required to move (or change) it. In this case, the motivating energy comes from the amount of resources that you commit to the initiative. The faster you want the initiative to accelerate, the broader the involvement required to motivate it. Resistance to its acceleration is amplified by the number of initiatives you attempt to complete during the business cycle and also the rate of improvement in business performance that's desired (or required). In this description, Newton's formula of F=MA is modified from Force = Mass multiplied by Acceleration into *Force = Manpower multiplied by Actions*. Your actual "rate of acceleration" for the implementation will depend on how skillfully you balance the breadth of deployment with number of actions initiated.

Balancing energy and mass into a rate of improvement that's required by the strategic plan is the responsibility of the senior leadership team. Implementing too few actions (too little force) is as detrimental to success as burying the organization in initiatives (too much resistance). Each induces a different type of failure, and this is where Newton's third law applies:

"For every action, there is an equal and opposite reaction."

The diversion of too much manpower toward the strategic tasks will remove an equal amount of attention from your day-to-day activities and can induce tactical failure. Commit too few resources to the effort, however, and the strategy will remain stillborn. It's always a balancing act when shifting resources from the daily business activities toward strategic initiatives but the performance of your tactical imperatives (the ones that pay the bills) almost always must be sustained with a balance and timing that assures day to day success, and acceptable strategic progress.

When it comes to results, introducing excessive initiatives (mass) absent sufficient manpower (energy) will cause critical objectives to fall late or incomplete. Conversely, significant dedication of resources (energy) applied to an inadequate number of initiatives (mass) will leave parts of the organization dis-engaged from achieving the objectives and unable to participate, formulating a "drag" on the force component. The strategy then fails to gain sufficient momentum on its own. Both examples can leave people unmotivated, or even drive them to be dissatisfied and negative, presenting the leadership team with even bigger engagement challenges.

Preparing for Change

To ready the organization for your change initiative, first try to estimate the degree of change the new strategy will impose. Confirm your list of both the operational impacts, as well as the physical ones, in order to determine the level of preparation (planning, communication, and training) that's required to prepare employees to adopt the specific changes.

Performing an impact assessment similar to the example below will provide "directional," insight that doesn't need to penetrate to extreme levels of detail. These work better in the absence of hard data and because the assessment is far more observational, it merely needs to be close enough to initiate a first cut at resource deployment.

Look at the project list from a couple of different perspectives. Begin by ranking the list of things that *must* change (see chapter one), as equal in priority to activities associated with running the business on a daily basis. Next, look at each of the business functions and try to estimate the workload imposed by each of the following factors: 1) maintenance of tactical performance, 2) current or pending project assignments, and 3) processes that will be changing. It's effective enough to use approximate percentages of impact for each, as shown:

Function	Tactical Load	Project Load	Process Changes	Total
Leadership	75%	10%	15%	100%
Customer Mgmt.	90%	15%	15%	120%
Product / Service Delivery	90%	30%	20%	140%
IT (Info Management)	50%	20%	30%	100%
Human Resources	70%	15%	25%	110%
Finance	80%	20%	30%	130%

The sample estimates would indicate that four areas are potentially overloaded. Realistically, given the range of error possible in the directional estimates, the high totals for product service or delivery and finance would be the only concerns to act on. At this point, you should move to balance them through resource allocation, changes in program scope or timing, or deferring the pace of results.

Having estimated the impact to functional workloads, the senior team is now positioned to revisit the must-change list and attempt a different directional assessment for the level of mass each might represent. The only true estimate of mass is going to come from looking at how the initiatives will task each of the functions involved. Next, revisit the list of things that cannot change, introduced earlier, to look for the organizational energy required to keep those untouchables firmly in place. Do so by approximating the involvement required to sustain monitoring and metrics for each.

One of the more frequently identified attributes that cannot be changed is the need for a sales team to maintain its perceived "benchmark" level of service to the customer. On the provision the senior staff agrees that the actual performance value measures up as a benchmark, there would be two directional effects to the organization. First, it might suggest that no negative structural or staffing changes could be allowed to impact the sales team. Second, the team's participation in the new initiatives would be limited to avoid diluting its customer service task loads and compromising sales performance. Although customer service levels certainly have to be maintained or improved, allowing one function to have a lower level of participation or even to opt out of cross-functional involvement in the change initiative isn't a workable situation. With that, a compromise has to be reached.

It's important to understand the impact that the "must-change" and "can't change" lists can have on the initiatives and the organization (the mass). Adjusting resource requirements (energy) to achieve the desired rate of change (resistance) allows the organization to tackle the new strategy in line with the expectations of both the leadership and the organization.

Structure and Staffing - In the story, we performed two different exercises in order to further evaluate the organization's readiness to implement its new strategy. The first one is called "Structure" because the process evaluates the organizational structure with the intent to make it more effective. The process involves both an organizational level skills assessment and a strategic skills assessment. A Structure event takes some preparation and effort, because individual skills assessment by themselves aren't easy, and rolling them up to cover the entire organization is even more difficult. Once the two are thoroughly compared, it will produce a gap analysis that can be used to finalize your organizational development action plans.

The second exercise they performed was called "Staffing." In this review, the senior staff performs a 360-degree review of each salaried associate (or a group defined by your own organization). Its mission is to gain a better understanding of each associate's performance effectiveness, leadership potential, and development or improvement needs. This review will provide a valuable resource assessment that can prove useful when it comes time to flesh out the teams charged with the implementation of the strategic initiatives.

VIINIE

VIINIE is an acronym used to describe a change management process structured so that the key elements of communication and involvement are utilized to help build the engagement that supports your change initiative. VIINIE's components include **V**ision / **I**nform / **IN**volve / **I**mpact measurement / **E**valuate, review and refine. The process was created to provide a sequence of execution, as well as a refinement loop for managing the organizations engagement in your cultural change initiative. This supports our emphasis in chapter 2 about the essential need to communicate the vision. In the VIINIE model, the *vision* forms the basis for the information that will be communicated to the organization.

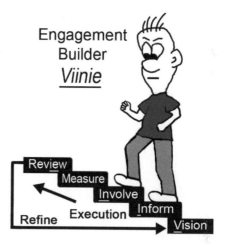

The engagement process begins by *Inform*ing the organization of the Vision through a comprehensive communication process that manages content, delivery, and timing. All three elements are required for the process to be effective, sustainable, and minimally disruptive. Its mission is to disseminate the correct amount of information to each level and function of the organization. In doing so, it should translate the vision into content that will make associates aware of both the internal and external reasons for the changes, the approach you'll be using to address them, who will be involved or affected, and what you expect to accomplish. If you can discern a hint of R=A+D in the method, you are correct! Effective communication of the vision goes a long way toward forming the "roots" of your associates' endorsement and participation.

As you begin communicating the elements of the strategy to the organization, keep them digestible in size—too much information at one time will not be effectively absorbed. Your messages must be crafted to reinforce the behaviors and encourage the actions necessary to achieve the strategy. Keep the messages in line with the way "Standard Work" is broken down in a Lean environment: Highly specified as to Content, Sequence, and Timing. As the implementation progresses, publicize the program status along with key learnings. Finally, always remember to treat communication and understanding, as separate tasks. Your goal is to create understanding, so don't let the act of communicating take precedent.

The *INvolve* step is much different. Because your choice of strategic initiatives will surely impose new demands on your organization and impress changes that will make some people uncomfortable along the way, it's best to start on the softer side. Tone down your emphasis on responsibilities, accountability, and expectations in the beginning. Instead, stress roles in the plan, as well as the changes in behaviors and relationships required to succeed. Always anticipate resistance (the *ready*), keep your early emphasis on the people and how the changes impact them (the *willing*), and do your best to simplify the technical solutions (the *able*).

Another element of the *Involve* step is a training and development plan designed to close the skills gaps that were identified as internal needs during the Structure session. This can rapidly open opportunities for high-potential associates and accelerate your ability to leverage the organization's adoption of the strategy. Carefully selected internal development candidates can have a far greater cultural engagement value and a shorter learning curve than might the typical outside hire.

Measuring Impact

People are responsive to what you measure; or are they? While they will generally respond to what gets both measured *and* monitored, timely reviews of progress on an initiative can help maintain the pace of activities, sustain organizational focus, and maintain the desired level of cultural engagement. Keeping associates thoroughly informed with regard to the nature of the strategy, while tasking them with activities that link directly to it, will retain their attention and their focus. Visible and active measurement, as well as follow-up on the progress of implementation, will keep them engaged.

Even though we introduced metric theory in chapter three, and will explore it more deeply in chapter eight, it's important to mention it here as a leveraging tool—more for engagement than simply to gauge performance. Used judiciously, impact measurements that include top-level public metrics, specific project measures, and personal targets, can all facilitate engagement. Organizations that master change succeed through relentless preparation not only for both the selection of initiatives and their targets, but also for their efforts expended to acclimate the organization to the strategy. Using separate measures for the engagement elements you deem critical to the execution of your strategy— associate development, organizational alignment, deployment of activities, etc.—is a foundational step toward managing the pace of cultural change needed to achieve the strategy.

The last steps in the VIINIE process, and the final element of preparation and managing change entail *Evaluate, review, and refine*. It's a lot to cram into only one letter of the acronym, but if I'd plugged all of them in, it just wouldn't have been a usable acronym. This step closes the "loop" of improvement because Evaluating your metric performance using *Review* cycles that utilize *live* results is more effective at guiding tactical adjustments in the *Refine* step. All of this should ultimately be fed back into the *Vision*. It's this use of active results to drive adjustments that knits engagement together and builds belief in the integrity of the process.

As the initiative progresses in step-by-step fashion, from communication of the vision to informing people of your expectations, involving them in the planning, execution, and assignment of tasks, your associates will engage in the process (see "pull behavior" coming up in Chapter 6). Maintain high visibility of metrics that are grounded in reality, represent visible progress, and that offer a public view of the strategy's status, conveying the drivers for refinements through the execution phase. Finally, you should do a consistent job of advertising success and celebrating it.

The Last Word

In setting an example for the "new" culture in your change initiative, there are some leadership behaviors that will help you. First, once you have committed resources to an initiative, take great care before you divert them in another direction; doing so sends a confusing message. When you have to, make the changes and the reasons public and acknowledge the impact. Second, always seek and accept feedback. You may not always be able to act, but just listening and (possibly) responding will leave a big impression.

Again, A.J. Sheppard captured this point well in his book "The Incredible Transformation of Gregory Todd:":

"Some of those who are resisting change most strongly are only doing so because they care. They're the ones you need to be listening to."

Preparation for change takes careful consideration for the magnitude of its impact on the organization, the changes in skills required, and in the level of involvement it demands. Taking this on without a specific *Approach*, or without understanding the intended *Results*, will leave gaps in *Deployment*. With a good situation assessment completed, engagement momentum is accelerated by keeping associates on the "inside" and informed, rather than being "left out in the cold." This avoids unnecessary conflicts between the strategy and the culture. You must continually work to keep the plan *live* because of its ability to affect people; and that directly impacts morale and culture.

Chapter five will introduce a different twist on how to sort through your priorities in a way you might not have imagined, and brings to mind another old adage: "When you have alligators snapping at your heels, it's hard to remember that your task was to drain the swamp." In those kinds of real-life dilemmas though, both the swamp and the alligators have to be dealt with. How to do that is coming up.

Chapter 5: Sorting Through the Dangers

Realistic Priority Management

Things that can Kill You!

1. **Mastering Priorities**

2. **Things That Kill You**

3. **Things That Can Eat You**

4. **Things That Make You Happy**

Squarely in the midst of rolling out the first of our newly identified strategic initiatives, our largest and most loyal customer called us to request an urgent meeting at their headquarters. We dutifully interrupted our planning sessions to assemble a team of key leaders and customer representatives for the trip.

Upon arrival, we were led to a large conference room already full of their people, with seating locations for our contingent assigned by name. Every one of the customer representatives remained seated as we entered. We moved in courteously and found our seats.

After a brief round of introductions, Mark, the company's president rose to address us. "We have been a key customer of yours for nearly half a century. To some extent, and for a variety of reasons, we've protected you as our sole supplier in your product category. Lately, however, your poor performance has begun to cost us business and is disrupting our own objectives. The situation has recently degraded to a point that we're no longer willing to tolerate it. Our purpose for inviting you this morning is to provide that proverbial 'shot across your bow,' and serve notice of the need for you to elevate your performance to a minimally acceptable level within the next ninety days. If you cannot, we will have no choice but to transfer twenty-five percent of our business with you to the next most appropriate supplier, one who also happens to be your main competitor. Today, we're willing to work with you to define a mutual set of performance objectives that will meet our minimum requirements, as well as to establish our expectations for rapid and significant progress on the key issues."

Even with my short association in the business, I knew we should have expected something like this. It's hard to describe the knot in my stomach as he ended his comments, but it was obviously my turn to step up and speak. Since we were keenly aware of the impact our performance problems were having on this particular customer, we had anticipated a discussion like this and had prepared a response, and I felt confident of the quality of the plan we were going to offer.

"First, let me thank you for the opportunity to be here. We recognize that we have given you every motivation to pull your business from us. The fact you're giving us an opportunity to maintain our long-standing business relationship is a reflection of your commitment to us as your business partner and it is sincerely appreciated. I promise you we will not waste this chance. I would like to make you aware of the extent to which a number of your concerns have already been identified and are being addressed in our operating plans for the coming year. Nevertheless, we will need to return to those initiatives and accelerate them in order to provide the improvements you require in a timeframe that will support a renewal to our relationship." My response seemed to satisfy most of their contingent.

"We all appreciate your commitment and are confident you'll achieve the objectives we set for you today, or we wouldn't have called this meeting," Mark said optimistically. "*But* I would like to get everything in writing so that nothing is left to miscommunication."

"I understand," I said. "My team and I are ready to start right now."

True to his word, the balance of the meeting was spent reaching an agreement on the improvements we would be held accountable for at the end of the ninety-day grace period. We left the meeting troubled over the magnitude of the challenge ahead of us, but equally relieved that our customer had the courtesy to give us a chance to improve our performance. It rarely happens that way.

Although we had just recently hosted this company's CEO in our strategic offsite planning sessions, he had failed to impart either the same sense of urgency or the condensed timeline that had just been impressed upon us by his president Mark. Many of their concerns regarding improvements in delivery and quality were already accounted for in our strategy deployment plans as were order entry and customer service enhancements. Regrettably, it was clear that our strategic timelines wouldn't generate enough improvement in time to meet the ninety-day deadline, and a new set of tactical actions would be required.

We needed to adjust our priorities quickly, and although all of us wanted to sustain the positive momentum we enjoyed during our strategic deployment process, it would have to take a back seat to this. Once we concluded the meetings and returned to our offices, we reconvened for a late evening planning session.

"Well, folks, we have three months to salvage our relationship with our biggest customer," I said. "That's no secret. The issue at hand is, are we united in *believing* we can make it happen?"

"I think we're all clear on what we need to accomplish, but probably not the path to achievement," Geoff said, as heads nodded in unified agreement.

It had been a long day, but I pressed on. "I would like to suggest that we take a little different angle on this in order to garner the right level of attention. I want each of you to create two lists. Develop one for all of the active projects and critical daily responsibilities in your areas. Then I want you to suggest a unique way that each of your individual functions can contribute directly to this performance turnaround. We can then come back together in the morning and work on them. Any questions?"

There were no questions, probably because everyone was exhausted, so we broke up and went home.

We all had to sleep fast, because the next morning came far too quickly. To help everyone get their heads clear and the lists completed, I let the second round of discussion wait until mid-afternoon to give them some additional time. As they came into the conference room one by one, there was clearly a lot of stress in everyone's eyes.

"Okay, let's get started. A long time ago, as I started to manage large projects with multiple moving parts, it became very difficult for me to establish a useable priority list. There were always initiatives on the timeline, and tasks on the list, and they didn't always fit together. One day, I came up with an idea to segregate my priorities into three groupings that is still used to this day. The first group was called, *'Things that will kill you!'* The description alone makes it obvious they would have to be addressed with the utmost urgency and focus. The roots of our own customer issues fall into that category because if we lose twenty-five percent of their business, we'll really be hurting. But there are other duties we need to recognize as well. Sometimes day-to-day activities will need to carry the same weight: transacting scrap, receiving inventory, paying employees and suppliers, and much more. If these aren't done on a timely basis, the business itself will spiral out of control."

"What about Engineering changes?" John asked

"Those are a solid maybe, depending on the implementation parameters and impact to the business or customer base." I answered. "'Things that Kill You' are typically rapid and high in impact, accumulating into big trouble quickly. The second priority group is called *'Things that will eat you.'* These are trickier because they are often more amorphous, eating you one day and killing you weeks later. My own favorite of these is scrap, because it might be very low level on a day to day basis, but when you roll it up over long periods of time it can accumulate to become a significant issue. One of our problems with this customer is quality, and the biggest quality issue they have is also one that is a recurring scrap problem in the factory. Normally with an 'Eater' we'll just throw some additional cost at them to get containment until we've crossed enough of the killers off the list, then return and fix them."

"Sounds kind of like triage," said Geoff. "When I was taught first aid in the Army, we were coached to handle the gaping wounds first, the serious but not life-threatening problems second, and let the cuts, bruises, and scrapes pretty much handle themselves."

"Not a bad comparison," I agreed. "One downfall to 'Eaters' is that you can get too used to putting them off, so you have to set review periods to stay honest about their placement on the list.

"Finally, there is a third level of priority items most appropriately called *'Things that make you happy,'* and they are, in essence, things like the strategic projects that we can and will set aside for at least 90 days. They might be important to the business, but relative to the other two more immediate priorities, they simply have to wait."

"Don't some of these corporate initiatives fall into the 'happy' category? They might make someone happy, but that person isn't in this room." Maria was on a bit of a roll.

"Well, we can discuss them, but we'll probably have to leave them in because the corporate office is also a customer of ours. If they are too much of a resource drain though, I'll go to bat to gain some relief for us. Okay, the floor is open. What else do you have?"

"You know, I obviously couldn't say this in the meeting yesterday, but our customer is at least partially responsible for some of our delivery problems by the way they forecast and order," Janet said softly.

"Anyone have an idea on how to respond to Janet's comment?" I asked.

"I hate to say it, but we might have to adjust our planning and production inventory to be capable of responding to any possible needs that may arise within their typical ordering timeframe. Even the unreasonable ones," Geoff ventured.

"Precisely," I concurred. "I believe it's our Response-Ability!"

"Why don't we make this customer a priority for all of our resources—in other words—give them preferential treatment?" Maria suggested.

I shook my head. "No, that's never seemed like the right thing to do, at least to me. Picking between our customers might solve the problems of one, but other problems are more likely to pop up with another. In a way, we would just be pushing the problem around and risking the alienation of other customers—the old carpet and bubble adage. Solving the problems of all of our customers requires a systemic solution that will be more sustainable. We need to review our systems and adjust them to get some honest short-term improvement, even if it's at some cost.

"Okay!" I continued. "Please try to categorize your list the way we just discussed, then we'll see just what we're faced with in the short term."

Once they had completed the categorization and we had discussed some rearrangements as a group, we moved on to the second list.

"Now, let's go to the *how you can help* list." I started them off. "Because the lion's share of the problems center around delivery and quality, let's leave Dick and Geoff for the end. We'll start with the support teams."

"I discussed this with my team this morning. We decided that we can relax some of our restrictions around the hiring of temporary employees to give you more ability to match workforce with demand," Maria started.

"I could also really use some help with hourly and salaried overtime management. Some of my supervision is new and aren't working by the rules the way they should." Geoff requested.

"You've got it," Maria answered. "Either myself or a team member will sit in on your overtime planning from here on.

"I think we can add some buffer inventory in critical areas that will allow us to be flexible with their lack of forecast accuracy. I hate to add inventory though," Janet said.

"More inventory isn't usually my answer either, but until we solve a few other things, it might be the right thing to do," I offered in support.

"We have already implemented active monitoring of some of their key quality indicators. Much of what they see as rejects, is not what we see internally. Clearly we need to adjust our expectations to match theirs and review what we're doing until we get to the root cause." Jerry, from the quality team, stated. His boss John nodded approvingly.

"And I will meet with my team to see if we can start to get ahead of their needs by mining some market intelligence and giving them faster responses to their inquiries." Dick didn't seem to be in the best mood over his commitment.

"These are all great! Can I get Accounting to put together a daily impact report? We need to cover daily changes in order levels: shipments, inventory receipts, labor spend, and customer returns."

"It will take a team effort, but I think we can come up with something," Jolene consented.

"Good! Then I'll look for responses to any abnormalities in the report before 9:00 am each day.

"Now, as to the containment activities," I said, "we need to conduct them on a cost-is-no-object basis to make sure they fully contain the quality and order management issues. That way they can drive an immediate impact to the customer. But we'll also need a feedback loop to ensure that we can take decisive action to quickly mitigate the cost problem with an effective solution."

"Why don't we establish a cross-functional containment team to work through the details?" Janet said. "I think Geoff and I should co-champion it."

"Great! As you do so, make sure that you record any and all related data so that we can assign a second team to drill down to the root causes of those issues," John suggested. "Then they can also take the lead on implementing the improvements."

"That's an awesome approach!" I could barely contain my excitement. "It should really help minimize the duration and cost of the containment activities. Please be sure to recognize each member of the team and give them an appropriate level of reprioritization. Don't let any other killers drop through, even though this gets top priority."

With the final list completed, we pulled up the project plan for customer performance improvement from the strategy sessions and expanded the team for an emergency session in an effort to turn our new-found sense of urgency into fast but accurate action. It was important for the entire organization to get engaged in this plan, and that employees understand the reasoning for the delays in some of the strategic initiatives that we've just kicked off. Through the course of our meeting, we revised the problem statements, timing, and project lists for the initiatives being accelerated, and revised the timing on the projects we knew would be pushed out. From there, we commandeered a war room and scheduled series of daily meetings in order to drive our containment actions for immediate implementation and monitoring. Placing the process on the war room wall and making it *visual* also had value to the other associates, as they could sense the common urgency, and see the actions, effort, and timing requirements for themselves. These would set a format for containment of the customer issues, while at the same time providing data for use in establishing our continuous improvement actions.

You're in a swamp surrounded by alligators. The water is too shallow to swim in and the bottom is too mucky to run. How do you decide what to do? The first thing you have to consider is that the alligators could kill you, and if getting away isn't a real option, you'll either need to outsmart them or find a way to defend yourself. With every move they make, you're fighting panic, and frantically looking for options. You're also getting increasingly worried about the ones you can't see, and your senses are alive to feel if you can detect one coming from underneath the water's surface. Time isn't your enemy, for every motion might contribute to their aggression. Any move you make must be calculated to improve your defensive position. You look around to see if they're moving toward you, but they appear to be stationary, checking to see if you are either a threat, or possibly dinner. What do you do?

Mastering priorities

In 1943, psychologist Abraham Maslow developed his view of man's "Hierarchy of Needs." His classification of essential human needs began with survival and evolved through safety, security, social needs, and self-esteem before ending with self-actualization. I studied Maslow a bit in college, and his theories had a definite impact. As my experience in the business world accumulated, I developed a hierarchy of my own. It was influenced by Maslow's thinking, yet entailed a simplified but dramatized approach to categorizing and establishing priorities for the organizations under my leadership. My personal hierarchy developed around the prioritization of business improvement initiatives and had only three levels for determining what to work on and in what order.

Establishing and sustaining priorities is a far different endeavor at the organizational level than it is at a personal one, primarily due to the number of individuals affected. Viewed personally, you have considerable control over the factors by which you rank and address your priorities, with the exception of any external interference (which I'm excluding but not discounting). At the organizational level, however, the priorities you establish as a leader will face exponential challenges. The formula goes like this:

$$\text{Priority execution} = \frac{\text{Organizational engagement (\# people)}}{(\text{\# of people involved x Internal initiatives) x External Issues}}$$

Got it? The equation isn't an attempt to quantify prioritization numerically, but rather it simply attempts to recognize and assign magnitude to the array of influences that can dilute the attention of your associates, potentially by being distracting enough to cause them to work on the wrong things. Keeping projects correctly prioritized helps them to stay focused on the most critical objectives. The dramatic nature of the descriptions used in my priority hierarchy are intended to stimulate people into making better choices. Let's start by describing all three more fully before we delve into how they influence each other.

"Things that Kill You" were named as such to emphasize the imminent peril of their negative consequences. These possess an ability to severely disrupt or disable a business, and they can come from many directions: problems with large customers, poor cash flow, or product and

service quality spills, major workforce events. Killers require fast and assertive action focused around containing their damage before you can even think about controlling or correcting them. One of the most perilous side effects of a killer is its ability to become all-consuming of the organization's attention and resources, placing at risk many other activities that are also on the must do list. Going forward, I'll refer to these as either TTKYs or "Killers" for short.

The next level of priority includes *"Things that Eat You."* These problems have a more erosive effect, differing in both pace and impact from the calamity-creating Killers. Eaters derive their name from the tendency to degrade performance over a longer period of time, having a more cumulative effect. They can sometimes be inconspicuous, subtle, and, much like a disease, they can be easy to overlook or ignore. Perhaps because of the low visibility of their consequences, or due to their slow rate of effect, organizations frequently fail to address them, consumed with working on greater urgencies (like Killers). With time, Eaters have the potential to grow into Killers if not contained and corrected. I'll refer to these as TTEYs or "Eaters" from here on.

The last group of priorities consists of *"Things that Make You Happy."* These belong at the top of the pyramid—near to the self-actualization level as Maslow described it. They are priorities that, while potentially important to the business, fail to address (either directly or indirectly) any Killers or Eaters that might be present. Although everyone loves to work on high profile "future" programs that bring such enjoyment, pursuing them at the ignorance of other issues that could destroy or damage a business is simply an exercise in denial. Since happiness is a requirement that necessarily must come after the avoidance of being killed or eaten, these should be worked on only after the first two are eliminated or when the Killers and Eaters are sufficiently contained and resources are still available to allow for it. One key reason for classifying TTMYH's as such is because their performance impact is usually longer term, more strategic in nature. More often than not they are consuming current resources (cash flow, time, capacity, etc.) for future returns. It's their own inability to generate enough short-term improvement to offset their consumption of resources that prevents them from ascending to the head of the priority list, even when their long-term impact might be significant. We'll refer to these as "Happys" going forward.

Again, this approach to classifying priorities has always been an effective way to command people's attention. The graphic nature of the terms is an important tool in helping employees maintain focus and sort through their own activities.

Let's look on how each type of priority affects the business on a day-to-day basis. Killers rightfully garner most of the organization's attention and all of its sense of urgency. The immediacy and severity of their impact creates a mandate for urgent response. Killers can be highly complex problems, or simple ones disguised by a set of complex circumstances; both are very difficult to resolve. Killers usually demand rapid and potentially costly action to contain the problem in order to protect the customer and the business. Once containment is achieved, it's imperative to perform a thorough assessment of the potential root causes in order to determine and implement the right permanent corrective action(s).

An example corrective process is what I call the three Cs: contain, cause, correct. This technique suggests that you must quickly isolate the list of potential causes and contain them so they are either stopped at the origin or kept within the business without being released to the customer or market. With effective containment in place, you can move resources to work on root cause or corrective action work using good disciplined problem-solving tools. When a solution is uncovered, deploying it as quickly as is practical will speed your recovery, hopefully moving it from Killer status, benefitting both the business and its customers. The negative impact of a Killer can take many forms: lost customers and market share, sudden drops in business levels and lost revenue due to pesky quality or shipment issues, quality-related problems that have exponentially negative potential (recall or liability costs), the loss of supply for critical business needs, or even just the erosion of profitability. These are areas where a significant and sudden negative change can endanger your market or operations so severely as to be almost unrecoverable. Although a Killer can sneak up on you, your response, commitment of resources, and drive for improvement must be sufficient to neutralize the potentially negative consequences.

Killers are the most difficult of the three priority levels to work through the 3 C's. Many organizations become proficient at containment and root cause but lose focus or are diverted away before completing the permanent corrective actions. These behaviors can become pervasive, yielding a culture that is reactive or even jumpy, consistently failing to close out problems and spending excessive amounts of time in fire-fighting mode. There are times when the containment alone can leave an organization so "out of breath" that it will struggle to attend to its daily business.

Eaters can be nearly as lethal as Killers, but their rate of attack is usually much slower, leaving their causes and the resultant damage lurking far enough below the organization's radar that they're often ignored. While the existence of an Eater can be painful, it rarely conveys the level of immediate threat that a killer does. Because of this, Eaters won't attract the attention or resources that a Killer will. Also, because of its covert profile (analogous to cancer), it can be a much easier decision to sacrifice some short-term performance and keep the organization focused on greater urgencies, such as its Killers. A former boss of mine used to say, "It's more important to stop the patient on the gurney from bleeding to death than to splint his broken leg."

Beyond the fact that their slow rate of attack can sometimes lull one into thinking they are only a nuisance, there is one other critical characteristic of an Eater helps them stay low on the priority list. Some Eaters are confusing, lacking a clearly apparent root-cause which often convinces people who are aware of them that they are normal—perhaps they are supposed to be there. They might over-estimate the resources required to correct them and can be justified against their visible or confused return on investment. The higher levels of urgency and visibility commanded by the Killers will usually shove Eaters to the back seat, and the presence of a high number of Killers might even push them off the list entirely.

Some examples of Eaters include dropped calls in a call center, order cancellations, unclear service diagnostic results, manufacturing scrap, process yield problems, and field failure rates. Let's look at an example of an Eater that can quickly migrate into a Killer. You're having account servicing problems that are affecting all of your customers, but they've led to cancellations only among some of your smaller clients, masking the overall impact. So far, the issue hasn't been significant enough to draw attention and the revenue impact has also been negligible. As a consequence, the root causes of the problems haven't been getting much attention. Suddenly, you're called on the carpet by a major account, who notifies you of the company's intent to cancel its business due to the same problems that have been eating away at the lower-level customers. Now, the issue has become such a threat to near term business performance that it vaults itself into the Killer category.

Another example is out of the automotive parts business. An assumed low-level quality yield problem within a manufacturing location suddenly appears in the field as a compromise to long-term product reliability; almost instantly, the component becomes a subject of a potential recall. Again, the cost of correcting the problem in the field is exponentially greater than that of containing or correcting it in the factory, and the issue jumps priority levels instantly.

Because of their elusive causes, the high effort required to correct Eaters can be driven by difficulties posed in chasing, isolating, and correcting them, or even by the extensive process driven solutions they might require. It's not uncommon for their causes to appear to come from multiple directions and to have a cumulative impact, necessitating extensive data gathering and analysis before it's even possible to plan your corrective action. As the data accumulates, the business impact becomes clearer in terms of cost, resources, and time requirements, at which point prioritization can be assigned more intelligently. Resource and time intensive tools, such as Six Sigma's DMAIC (Define, Measure, Analyze, Improve, Correct) or the logical problem-solving approach of PDCA (Plan, Do, Check, Act) are useful when in search of the root causes. Culturally, the problem with Eaters is that appearance is everything, and their appearance allows them to be underestimated in some way and allows *all* attention to be quickly drawn toward any present Killers. Focusing on only the visible impact just leaves you with "iceberg syndrome," since the damage caused by Eaters is usually greater below the waterline.

Even though Happys should always be last, they might wander onto the middle of the priority list for a number of reasons. For one, their strategic value might be subjectively inflated above the value of other near-term activities. A project that is more strategic in nature generally suggests a short-term benefit that's less than other more rapidly implemented tactical programs. The truth is that we are sometimes happy to divert resources from those higher value programs if the perception of value is in error. A second reason might be that they offer psychological relief from the stress of more immediate urgencies since they tend to be more positive and forward looking than the more perilous Killers and Eaters. It could be a conscious decision to jump a Happy ahead in priority just to seek relief from the stresses of higher-pressure priorities.

Happys can be a capital investment, a social or benefits program, or even a tempting acquisition opportunity. It might even be a customer account that isn't concentric to the core business. All of these can be falsely elevated in priority, even when they don't really link to a near-term need. Happys can also find their way into the middle group any time they get a leadership sponsor, so it takes some discipline to keep them in their proper place.

However you choose to identify them, it's wise to set them aside to prevent them from draining resources from your Killers and Eaters. It could accelerate their own negative effects before you're even aware of the conflict.

Because they are usually easy to identify, sorting and classifying your Killers and Happys on the priority list can be quickly accomplished. It's the Eaters in the middle that require the most scrutiny, since they might be Killers in disguise. As we stated, the risk of letting Happy projects into the middle lies in the diversion of critical resources away from more critical problems. Allowing a Killer into the middle can be disastrous—particularly if it's pushed there by an excessive number of them. If that happens, you should consider assigning outside resources to assist in their containment and correction as quickly as possible.

For every issue, it's important to identify the key business- and customer-facing process breakdowns that contribute to the problem and push them onto the corrective action list. From there, improvement efforts supported by the orderly collection, arrangement, and review of the pertinent data. The best approach can vary depending on the challenge, but taking a high-level view of the business with the use of process- or activity-mapping tools is often a great place to start. Fill them out with data to see how things are flowing—products, cash, sales closures, and engineering programs. Add any known error or defect rates to better understand what's dropping through, and integrate the results into the review to estimate the resources and time required to fix each matter. I always like to say, *"Do the math!"* With the starting points identified, establish your priorities and execute the plan *as quickly as you can!*

So, we've arrived at the midpoint of the book, having covered vision, Response-Ability, R=A+D simplicity, change management, and prioritization. All of these core concepts were arranged to define and address the "what" for your tasks ahead; the remaining chapters are structured to help you sort through the "how."

Chapter 6 deals with helping associates understand how to respond to a business issue once they've recognized its presence. We'll talk about how to use "pull behaviors" to support a compelling engagement motive.

Stephen Covey once said:

"The bottom line is, when people are crystal clear about the most important priorities of the organization and team they work with and prioritized their work around those top priorities, not only are they many times more productive, they discover they have the time they need to have a whole life."

It just makes sense, doesn't it? If you set a team-based, clearly articulated direction and maintain the course as closely as possible, everyone wins! Don't let the things that eat you accumulate until they kill you! Start working ahead of them now!

Chapter 6: "Pull Start" Your Transformation

Using "Pull Behaviors" to Trigger Team Achievement

1. **Pull Behaviors**

2. **Blame *ME*, Please!**

3. **Request**

4. **Provide**

5. **Guide**

As we began to tackle the containment activities we'd identified to resolve our immediate customer challenges, it became clear that those solutions would have to be more than just systemic (planning, execution, and quality related). For us to improve our product and services performance, there were obvious cultural/behavioral issues enabling our problems to be more severe than they should be, and would have to be addressed. In order for us to move as quickly as possible, we divided our efforts between the leadership team and the balance of the management staff. While the functional teams went to work containing the systemic issues, the leadership team explored the behavioral elements that were exacerbating the problem.

"In order for us to achieve our improvements quickly enough, we'll need to unearth the organizational behaviors that are impairing our performance at Valhalla Product Solutions and then develop a plan to change them as rapidly as possible. To accomplish that, we'll first need to figure out how to identify them. Does anyone have any ideas?" I looked back at the team, trying to gauge their non-verbal responses.

"We need to focus on this important customer!" Dick responded emphatically.

"But I'm afraid if we focus on just the one customer the entire effort will be viewed as a fire drill and the cultural impact won't last." Maria's response was right on point.

"The insight reflected in your comment is very astute, Maria," I said. "Deferring to an example out of my own experience in Lean Enterprise, it seems our folks would tell us that we need to be totally focused on all of our customers. Do we think a solution that focuses on only one specific customer can fulfill that broader commitment?"

"Of course we don't," Janet quipped. "Or we'd already be servicing everyone exactly the way they want us to."

"So, isn't a comprehensive list of customer dissatisfactions the first objective to establish, along with the set of behaviors that we need to change?"

"Sure it is, I guess." Dick sounded tentative.

"Okay, so if the behavioral result we want is for everyone in the organization to become more customer-focused, then we need examples of both positive and negative behavior from the people who are customer facing or involved in fulfillment, right?" Janet offered me the perfect setup.

"Maybe, but if we ask for certain behaviors from those who directly service the customer, and someone in a support role doesn't have the same level of commitment, won't it break down?" I asked them.

"So, we need everyone in the organization to be customer focused." Karen was thinking out loud.

"Why don't we just get them into an all-employee meeting and tell them what's going on so that they understand the situation and have a chance to buy in? Geoff asked

"I don't think that will be enough," I answered. "We'll need to employ a second key principle of Lean and engage them in the solutions."

"How do we do that?" John, from the engineering team, asked. "Particularly with my guys, who rarely interact with the customer and probably won't get the chance. Some of them barely take their eyes off of a computer screen during the day, here or at home."

"There is some facet of every employee's daily responsibilities that impacts our ability to service our customers! We can put together a customer impact list that touches every individual's job and then employ another Lean-based technique I've used called 'pull behaviors' to help them through the solutions," I answered. "It can leverage a compelling and personal reason for each and every associate to commit to customer satisfaction. Typically, the external customer support needs go without saying, but introducing the concept of internal customers often helps them to visualize how their internal behaviors ultimately link up to impact our external performance. This helps to 'root' their personal responsibilities in the end game. As an example, if an accounting procedure is indirectly causing an order to be late, all involved parties need to engage to enable the process to perform within the customer's time requirements, not ours."

Maria was clearly intrigued. "I'm interested in seeing how that will work."

"We need to demonstrate that they can personally impact the situation, and to do so we have to start *with* them," I responded. "A good place to begin might be to interview our customer-facing associates to see what barriers prevent them from responding to the customer with the correct answer or the right timing. From there we can connect the dots to the people and processes that support them, showing each team where to take corrective action so they can move at the *customer's need for speed.* Who wants to make a recommendation as to where we start?"

"I agree that we should start with the customer-facing associates," Dick said. "They are constantly running into problems trying to get their jobs done."

The rest of the team agreed, and having reached consensus on a starting point, we broke into two teams and adjourned. One group headed off to work on the customer facing people and another to tackle the support groups. We moved through the organization quickly, talking to people about their performance barriers with the primary objective of understanding:

1. What were the obstructions to servicing our customers in the response time they required?

2. What impact might they personally have on the improvements?

3. What, in their opinion was the first step they would personally take to fix it?

It didn't take very many face-to-face discussions for us to realize that while everyone in the organization uniformly cared about servicing our customer, many associates felt helpless to correct the problems that were hurting performance, because most of the causative factors seemed to be outside of their control. Furthermore, it became clear that many of our processes had developed their own individual performance targets, most of which were disconnected from the goals we had recently identified for the business.

With the customer-facing interviews completed, we reconvened to summarize what we learned.

"It seems that the biggest issues facing the account managers involve the timing of quote completions, pricing approvals, and delivery commitments. A lot of times customers will call us at the last minute and want a response the next day—it's usually based on a need that has popped up." Dick started us off.

"There is a lot that goes into that. When a special request comes in and has to be engineered, quoted in either the plant or through procurement and rolled into the schedule; they can't expect one-day response!" said Janet. John mumbled concurrence.

"But are there things we can do to fast track it? Maybe we can separate the easy requests from the difficult ones, and then allow a standard response time." I was trying to keep them calm and thinking.

"Since many of the delays end up on Accounting's desks, I think we can take the lead in doing that," said Jolene. "We can designate a time limit for both types of response and then set up a monitoring process to make sure that people are aware of the time limits. Awareness facilitates response!"

Because many of the causes of delays were considered to be by-products of our product and service delivery processes, it became clear that the fastest way to gain traction on the issues would be to engage associates to redesign and change those processes in order to make a difference. "How" to do this in a very controlled approach was still the challenge.

Our first step was to communicate to them frankly and honestly about our current status with our customer and the potential impact of not achieving their mandates. We shared what we learned through the course of the interviews and presented the information in a way that honestly framed our "burning platform for change." From there, we presented our own management contract: a list of guaranteed outcomes from the interview sessions and renewed responsiveness commitments on the part of the leadership team. Lastly, we closed with a short list of our expectations (mostly behavioral), requesting their assistance in continuously identifying the issues, as well as their participation in developing the targeted solutions. In general, they responded favorably to the thoroughness of our approach and the unprecedented level of open communication; we had harnessed their attention and built interest and excitement around the possibility for success.

Although we took steps to place a few non-business-critical issues on hold, for the most part, we asked the team to volunteer their participation in developing the solutions. Our management contract listed the specific areas where certain short-term expectations would give way to the successful resolution of the customer issues.

With the engagement and motivational momentum building, we reconvened the functional leadership teams and set to work designing the process solutions.

"Behavioral pull requires each process to have a 'trigger' mechanism that alerts the associate who is responsible for that process of the need for action," I began. "These 'triggers' can be tied to a specific problem occurrence or abnormality, or can request a response that covers a group of possible issues. Associating a specific 'trigger' to a single problem makes it easier to train for, while a trigger that covers multiple issues can require at least two levels of training. Once you've identified the type of trigger and number of issues it should address, your training design should equip every one of the associates charged with running the process to provide the correct solution. Can someone think of an example?"

"I would think the best triggers would either be visual or audible." Jeremy, one of our engineers, offered. "In fact, different triggers might be used to *request* a response from the cell operators, or to call for outside assistance. I can see lights and sirens for certain machine functions or process logjams that the associate would correct, but also possibly a different set of lights to alert maintenance, engineering, quality, or the management team."

"Great!" I jumped in. He was definitely getting the gist of the process. "Let's set you loose to make lists of all of the triggers you can think of for each process, and the training needed to implement them.

"There are a couple of other aspects of the process beyond the triggers that are important. We will need to identify who is responsible to *provide* the response to a given trigger. And finally, we'll need to develop work instructions that can *guide* them through best response to potential abnormalities."

The team proceeded to brainstorm visual indicators to help people to recognize the existence of a number of problems, implementing them in several areas. Accounting put together baskets labeled 1-3, representing the age in days of a quote request, and a separate basket labeled "expedite." Any request that hit the "3" basket had to be completed without delay while the expedite basket required immediate review. Similar systems were put to work in procurement and engineering. In the factory, any items related to workflow, and also subject to constantly changing status (e.g. product quality, inventory levels, delivery of services, and order backups), were assigned response triggers created by the users themselves.

This approach provided multiple benefits. First, empowering the associates to design the triggers helped to expedite understanding and build ownership in their use. Second, the type of response needed also conveyed a visual element. Finally, the triggers were structured in such a way that the parameters or "boundaries" for decision-making were also visually supported, closing the loop of *requesting, providing, and guiding* the response. With the initial phase of the system complete, we were confident that any abnormal condition would receive the correct response in time to prevent them from reaching the customer.

One by one, we implemented similar systems for each of the business processes that the teams identified. Any abnormalities in those processes were quickly elevated in order to receive the appropriate attention, were corrected more rapidly than in the past, and became symbolic of the success of the overall approach.

For this chapter, I wanted to begin with a very astute quote regarding the subtle importance of culture. It goes without saying that cultures are difficult to change, but the impact of leadership—including leadership's priorities, set examples, and treatment of both customers and associates—cannot be underestimated.

"Culture guides discretionary behavior and it picks up where the employee handbook leaves off. Culture tells us how to respond to an unprecedented service request. It tells us whether to risk telling our bosses about our new ideas, and whether to surface or hide problems. Employees make hundreds of decisions on their own every day, and culture is our guide. Culture tells us what to do when the CEO isn't in the room, which is of course most of the time." Frances Frei and Anne Morriss

This chapter is about the methods and mechanisms that will influence your culture into making those discretionary decisions, mentioned above, in a way that is consistent with your chosen organizational philosophy. Behavioral Pull is not about automating response systems as much as it is about establishing both guiding principles and a clearer delineation of roles and responsibilities. It's use of engagement in the design of its systems is the differentiator that makes it powerful.

Virtually everyone with experience in Lean Enterprise or the Toyota Production System have used "pull systems" as a core method to manage how their processes respond to changes in demand. On a Lean factory floor, "pull" is most simply defined as make nothing until an external customer or downstream process (an internal customer) requests or "pulls" it. This is in contrast to the more wasteful "push" systems where an upstream process produces what, how much, and whenever it wants—regardless of what a customer actually demands.

Applied correctly in a sequential process environment, "pull" systems make for remarkably efficient processing, with minimal work in process, little wasted effort, higher quality, and production output that is closely linked to market consumption. This is the exact opposite of a push system, which consumes precious materials and resources (labor, capacity, and time) in a way that's out of step with customer needs, making timely supply of true market demand difficult or even impossible. Push systems always generate waste!

The leaders and implementers of Lean techniques in manufacturing and service businesses understand that no matter how simple the Lean tool kit is kept during implementation, establishing sustainable behaviors is always a challenge. Sometimes this occurs because one or more of the complimentary supporting tools aren't in use, exploiting one tool's co-dependency on another and causing them to break down. In nearly 25 years of experience implementing Lean and more than 30 years utilizing many of the tools that preceded it (Just-In-Time manufacturing, continuous flow, and others), the problem has proven to be pervasive. My own experience supports that the most difficult aspects of implementing Lean is in getting an organization to understand the following:

1. Many of the various Lean tools have inter-dependencies that benefit from parallel implementation.

2. Broad engagement is essential. Pocketed engagement only increases its tendency to suffer breakdowns.

3. When the need to respond to delivery and quality issues begins to take precedent over the normal operation of production and service fulfillment processes, the business has entered what I refer to as the "death spiral." If you're spending more time fixing problems than you are working on improving the business, you're losing the game. Sustainable behaviors simply will not take root in this environment.

In recent years we've emphasized the need to shift the focus of Lean implementation away from a tools-only based approach and toward the direction of managing the behaviors needed to implement and sustain improvements. How does an organization aspiring to cash in on the enormous benefits of a thorough Lean implementation and instill these behaviors in order to make its investment in time and training be sustained at the operating level? My answer to that is a simple one:

PULL SYSTEMS!

But not the kind of pull systems that move product or services along the delivery route to satisfy a customer, this is a different kind.

BEHAVIORAL PULL SYSTEMS!

"Behavioral Pull" applies some of the basic principles of Lean pull systems to the performance of your work teams. But even in its simplest form, Behavioral Pull is more complex than just making and using something. Behavioral Pull mimics the essence of the Lean Pull "need-respond" sequence by elevating the organization's ability to recognize the differences between normal and abnormal process performance and then provide the appropriate response.

The first step in establishing pull behaviors is to visually define normal versus abnormal for a given process or activity, because it isn't always obvious. Next, it's necessary to identify the organizational responses necessary to maintain a properly performing manufacturing or business process, as well as the list of responders or process owners. Finally, processes are redesigned to include built-in visual and instructional cues that will request the needed maintenance behaviors as well as the corrective problem responses for the specific abnormalities. In order for behavioral pull to work in the same way Lean Pull does, a request–to-response sequence should be broken down into separate components. These include the following components: *request* (a need trigger), *provide* (a trained, disciplined response to the defined needs), and g*uide* (visual and other instructions that support the correct response).

Blame *Me*, Please!

Nobody says that, do they? Pull behaviors are all about engagement and empowerment, but blame-oriented cultures create a strong undercurrent against successful empowerment. The cultural "reaction" to assigning blame in a situation invokes fault and immediately overrides the more correct assumption that most associates are trying to do both a good job and the "right thing" in the course of performing their work. When something goes wrong, the "who" involved can be an important data point in the pursuit of the root cause, but it's commonly feared because of the negativity of being associated with "what went wrong." In real life, most problems result from a blend of circumstances that can unfortunately place the individual at the center. Improper training, poor preparation, and preventable or unanticipated process problems are at fault more often than carelessness or malicious intent. Blame cultures will seek the person too quickly and *might* pursue the other causes afterward, or they might just stop there!

To begin moving your culture away from blame orientation, two things must happen. First, you should take assertive steps to separate blame from accountability, because it is possible to hold people accountable without invoking blame. Second, it's important to delay the assignment of responsibility for a problem until you've looked thoroughly at all of the underlying facts—especially when they aren't immediately apparent. Begin constructing the *"what"* (as in what happened) in painstaking detail by using a logic-based technique such as "5 Whys" and starting at the point that the problem surfaces. Even when some of the causative factors point to an individual, avoid jumping to the *"who"* until the end, after all of the "what" data suggests that you should. Once an individual's actions are actually determined to be a contributor to the causes, the corrective action should still focus on process construction, training, and error proofing before addressing individual performance (see chapter seven: Jidoka and Error Proofing)! These are viable techniques to eliminate the potential for human error without defaulting to the person You'll have to give people breaks in favor of a relentless pursuit of root cause in order to begin creating the desired culture and turning off the "blame-throwers."

Logical problem-solving techniques support blame elimination by discouraging what I call *"jumping to contusions"*: hasty or incorrect presumptions of root cause that end in wasted effort, pain, and difficulty, slowing the discovery of root cause through misdirection.

Jumping to "Contusions"

Disciplined root cause work can help to avert the defensiveness and apprehension that might otherwise impede the implementation of corrective actions. The use of work teams to identify and eliminate the specific problem cause(s) builds "forward ownership" in the solution, as well as a team-based environment that engenders behavioral support for the corrective process changes.

Using team-based, logical problem-solving techniques to clearly identify root cause, and supporting them with structured process-improvement tools to implement sound solutions, will assist you in cleansing blame from your culture. Keeping the organization focused on physical or procedural remedies as opposed to individual responsibilities also produces more sustainable solutions. To understand this better requires us to relate to a key concept of "Error Proofing": if a (process) defect has a statistical possibility of occurring, then it *will* occur. My analogy for this is "pollution in the stream" because although the problem may be so small that you might never be able to see it, the statistical potential for its existence means it *is or will be* there at any point in time. The sustainability of your solution depends on the extent to which it can eliminate every possibility of the problem occurring. One final thing, eliminating blame will make your problems solving efforts both more efficient and effective.

Recognizing Abnormalities

An associate's ability to provide a suitable and timely response is going to be highly dependent on his or her understanding of the difference between normal process operation and abnormal performance, as well as the factors that create each condition. Complex processes will have a variety of contributing factors that, when performing abnormally or below expectations, can require different responses. Each issue must be clearly defined and associated with a specifically trained response in order to sustain normal process performance.

Your processes should be redesigned so that the existence of an abnormality is readily and visually apparent. Associate training must enable them to recognize the trigger(s) associated with each problem and respond with a containment or corrective action. As noted above, normal process operating limits should be visually identifiable, as well as the response trigger points and the corrective actions necessary to return performance to target.

Request

So, let's look at how behavioral pull employs a "trigger" to request a specific "response" to any group of identified process abnormalities. The process design should incorporate a visual cue that exposes the problem as quickly as it occurs, hence the name "trigger." The trigger design will identify the issues and request intervention from the associate responsible for the process who will provide a corrective or containment action that is supported by their training. Using an example from a payables process: an abnormality occurring from an accumulation of too many pending accounts payable initiates a response request. The "trigger" designed by the team is a simple physical height gauge next to the payable's inbox which visually approximates the number of invoices waiting in cue. Once the stack reaches a height indicated by a color-coded mark on the gauge, additional associates, who are also trained to process payables, respond by shifting to the process—adding capacity and reducing the backlog.

Another example is in a manufacturing process where production activity is controlled by visual locations on the floor that instruct associates to start or stop the process based on the presence or amount of inventory in them. If the locations are filled, no product is to be produced, but if they are emptied and the markings are visible, their color codes (red, yellow, green) visually instruct the process operators on how much product to make as well as how urgently the response is needed. Yet another example might be a customer service process (you've seen this in large retail stores) where the number of people in line (possibly identified by markings on the floor, wall, or hanging from the ceiling) will trigger customer service associates to respond by moving from other activities to the backed-up checkout lines.

The common element of these behavioral requests is their use of visual or audible triggers to specifically expose the problem and request those associates assigned as responders to proceed as they are trained based on the abnormality. Finally, as we will explain in the *Guide* step, if the problem cannot be resolved by the associates assigned efforts and within a designated time period, their training should cue them to elevate the problem to the next level of process management.

Provide

With the abnormalities identified, the corrective actions defined, and the behavioral responses targeted, training is used to enable associates to recognize and respond correctly to a specific type of problem request. The extent of the training required is dependent on the complexity of the process, but it's important to point out that both training and "Response-Abilities" should be layered across the organizational levels to provide "tiered engagement" by everyone associated with the process. Whether the person is charged with operating the process and recognizing the existence of the issue, or supervising the area with responsibility to support and reinforce the response, it's this combination of training, the responsibility to escalate, and the visual controls that makes the organizational response to a process issue more "reflexive."

By "reflexive," I'm referring to a response that becomes "subconsciously automatic" from the respondent. You can't accomplish this kind of response in a single event, but you will build it with a combination of training and standardization that's sufficiently clear, thorough, and so well reinforced that the correct response occurs without external intervention. The more complex the process and the response required, the more frequently it should be reinforced. My own personal understanding of being "reflexive" came from a period when I was wrestling for a Division 1 university. Our coach would drill us on certain techniques until we were virtually sick of them. At the time, it seemed to be more punitive than beneficial. A few years after my competing career was over, I returned to the sport to coach my own sons. Even after so much time away, my ability to react to live situations with the correct technical responses surprised me. It had taken me that long to learn and appreciate that he'd trained us so thoroughly that our physical reactions had moved beyond a conscious decision to a subconscious response I like to call "reflexive."

Guide

Once your process controls are established, they should be visually integrated with their respective abnormality responses. User training will enable associates to provide the proper actions according to their visual cues. Making the process control elements visual is a fundamental principle of Lean, and, by default, of behavioral pull as well. The visuals support and strengthen the value of the training, helping to semi-automate a reflexive and repeatable response when a trigger activates. All of these contribute to your ability to sustain normal process performance.

With triggers that are designed to visually communicate as much information as is possible about the existence and nature of the issue, other process visuals will help to clarify who should respond and request the appropriate response. Again, the visuals are intended to solicit and support associate intervention for all aspects of process performance. This includes normal functions, flow controls for quality and rate of output, and intervention actions to counteract abnormalities, involvement, the timing or urgency of the response, and more.

Let's look at an example of a visually controlled customer service process:

| | Visual Controls | | Layers of "Pulled Behavior" | | |
	Normal	Abnormal	Associate	Supervision	Management
Service Flow	Customers in line equal 5 or fewer		Continue operation	Normal monitoring	Random monitoring—verbal
		More than 5 customers in line	Change lane light to yellow	Increased monitoring Support associate—redeployment; open a new lane	Increase attendant staff if problem persists
Problem Response	Service lane light is on—white in color		Continue operation	Monitor as appropriate	Random monitoring—verbal cuing
		Lane light is flashing Yellow	Available associates open a new lane	No associate available: Self-staff a lane or elevate w/intercom	Self-staff a lane or call in additional Associates

In the above example, visual cues are lighted (lane lights) or add an audible trigger (intercom). Each level of the organization is trained to provide a different response based on the type of cue.

Now, let's look at an example of a visually supported manufacturing process:

	Normal	Abnormal	Associate	Supervision	Management
Scheduling	Material present in Staging zones – raw (In)		Produce to schedule	Normal monitoring	Random Monitoring
		Empty in or out staging zones	Resolve and /or elevate	Resolve when elevated	Inquire when aware, involve as needed
Production/Flow	Process is operating (green		Produce to schedule	Normal Monitoring	Random monitoring
		Operation is ceased (red light)	Resolve problem or elevate	Respond to visual cue & resolve	Inquire when aware, resolve as needed
	Material present in staging zones —finished (out)		Continue operation under guidelines		
		Staging area is empty	Resolve or seek help	Ensure solution or help	Inquire /Involve as needed
Quality	Good product staged		Continue operation	Visual monitoring	Visual monitoring
		Products red-tagged on- hold	Seek assistance (red light)	Respond as cue requests	Be aware & involve as required

In this example, the cues include lighting and color-coded staging areas. The staging locations are designed to accommodate a limited amount of moving material with the requirement that, if they are filled, the process must stop. The general design of each of the cues and triggers is standardized across the organization, however, the cues vary by both the process and the type of problem, and response requests will typically be specific to them.

The management task associated with behavioral pull is to engage associate input and participation in the design of the visual controls, the responses, and also the guidance training. This helps them to contribute valuable knowledge and commit more fully to the program through the rules of response. On a day-to-day basis, management supports continuous improvement through sufficient resource allocation, priority management, layered auditing, and consistency of expectations. This last point is most critical because if the management expectations of the process become variable or you allow priorities to change excessively, your associates' ability to make good decisions will break down and the consistency of results will be lost. Like the rest of the organization, managers should be trained thoroughly in the use and meaning of the visual controls, their ongoing role in day-to-day reinforcement of them, and how to establish expectations that are consistent with the desired response. From a support perspective, the set of expectations must also require full participation in training from all levels of associates.

As a Manager, you can better establish a culture to support Pull Behaviors by doing the following:

1. Remove the drudgery from an associate's task load (using Lean Autonomation). Where possible, automating or eliminating the most repetitive job components allows them to shift their focus toward more critical process indicators—I call it "elevating their line of sight from the stripes on the road to the curve ahead." This elevated viewpoint makes their jobs more value-added by virtue of the additional responsibility.

2. Facilitate their awareness of process abnormalities, allowing them to be as proactive as their new capabilities will permit. While it increases the organizational stress on the need to train, it also frees associates to "see and respond," reducing the impact of common daily problems.

3. Involve them in the creation of the visual systems or triggers needed to operate the environment. Their participation will engender ready adoption of the techniques and the end result will be a culture that begins to embody the concepts of continuous improvement.

4. Empower them to respond and *avoid blame*! Creating a culture of response requires with clear definition of the actions needed in each situation, the time requirements for them to resolve the problem, and when they should elevate it and see assistance.

Now, in truth, "Behavioral Pull" does simulate a basic stimulus and response environment, but the reality is that the stimulus is automated by the visual arrangement and friendliness of the environment, while the response is the result of thorough skills training associated with specific conditions and by engaged associates.

While the concept itself was developed in manufacturing and services environments, the use of this process isn't limited to strictly those kinds of businesses. "Behavioral pull" can be employed anywhere that a repeatable customer response protocol is needed, and the results at the customer level can be astounding.

Summary

So, the visuals engage by exposing the problem and requesting intervention; training guides the response, enabling associates to reflexively provide the correct support to the trigger's request. Management commitment is demonstrated through support for the investment in training, the establishment of consistent expectations, and the monitoring of key performance indicators. The cultural impact of all of this is "pull behavior." Converting it back to R=A+D, the correctly-trained response is the desired result that comes from your approach through training, with responsibilities deployed to the associates who are expected to provide corrective action. Implemented thoroughly and with due patience, behavioral pull systems will improve response and engagement, paving the way to more timely problem resolution, and sustained higher levels of performance.

As is often the case, getting there requires starting small and building up. Beginning at the line management level helps you to attack a "hinge point" where your successes frequently break down and sustainment fails—the transition from vision to concept and into execution. This is where the process of changing the embedded behaviors of others will be supported or thwarted, so leveraging ownership by initiating your process improvements with them can be transformational. Once your line management has mastered their own response behaviors, they are ready to support movement to the next level and so on, level by level. In all cases, the Lean tools will, elevate the visibility of issues, and assist in the establishment of guidelines for correction. In the final stages of implementing "Behavioral Pull," the existence of a problem should be so obvious that the need for a corrective response is clearly visible and understood, even by an outsider.

But, what does it take to break it all down? The common mistakes made when trying to enlist engagement include: 1) underestimating resistance by failing to understand its origins within the involvement group; 2) trying to go it alone, or involving too few associates in the process design—flying "solo" ignores the teams knowledge, prevents their buy-in and reduces organizational momentum; 3) trying to solve the problem with only a technical solution, which rarely works when there is heavy influence by the human element; and 4) failing to celebrate success at the same pace as the achievements. Too little celebration suggests a lack of appreciation while excessive celebration can create the appearance of unwelcome hype.

While many organizations attempt to implement Lean, most fail to understand the application and inter-relatedness of the tools. To make matters worse, they assign responsibility for deployment to a few individuals whose influence doesn't extend broadly enough across the organization, and they struggle to generate and sustain improvement. The use of "Pull Behaviors" to engage more associates in providing a guided response to problems affecting the flow and quality of their work *will* be the differentiator between a successful Lean implementation and an attempt that merely looks lean. Dr. Aubri Daniels, Founder of ADI had a simple insight regarding this:

"We can change culture if we can change behavior!"

Chapter 7: *Takt*-ical Management

Using Lean Tools to Build Improvement

1. **The Lean Commandments:**

2. **Achieve Flow**

3. **Avoid Sub-optimization**

4. **Manage using Cycles of Response**

5. **Deploy the Lean Tools**

6. **Implementing Lean**

"Folks, I'd like you to meet Jorge Ribero," I said. "He's a Lean Enterprise expert whom I've asked to come in and help us gain some traction on improving the overall performance of our operations."

"Greetings, I will appreciate it if everyone here can arrange to meet with me at some point today," he spoke slowly, articulating carefully in spite of his thick Brazilian accent. "My evaluation will take only a couple of days. However, I need your opinions about the issues in your operation to help me suggest the correct solutions to your directors."

Several of the customer issues we highlighted during our strategy sessions and the ensuing corrective action team meetings were rooted to deeper problems that became apparent as we attempted to apply visual and behavioral pull solutions. The organization struggled with Lean Enterprise implementation for years, getting inconsistent results that were rarely sustained. Now, as they began to dig more deeply into several of the most pressing problems, it was clear that a more intense commitment to Lean would be a game-changer. Since their own Lean skillsets were thin and we had identified it as one of our critical strategies, it seemed wise to enlist outside expertise to help us determine the best course of action toward putting our Lean effort to work. Jorge and I were familiar with each other, and I knew his skilled observations would make a tremendous difference.

Jorge spent the better part of the next three days interviewing the leadership team, the functional managers, and key contributors, both to gain insight into some of our business practices and issues, as well as to evaluate whether we had any internal candidates capable of leading our Lean effort. Jorge meticulously combed through our manufacturing processes, asking questions, jotting notes, offering a few observations, and even taking some measurements. He was looking specifically for those areas where we could quickly improve the flow of our processes and generate an impact to all customers, not just our unhappy one. On the fourth day, we came together to hear his report.

"Some things you are doing very well, some not so well," he said, as he paced the conference room. On occasion his delivery would quicken, the thickness of his accent making him more difficult to understand. The meaning behind everything he said, however, was very clear. His delivery was as concise as if he had rehearsed it to maximize its efficiency.

"I have reviewed your production processes and spoken with your key people. Mostly, I see a good capability for you to perform Lean, without significant problems with attitude. Your employees have good work habits, but the quality of workflow is poor, and there would appear to be something like 15-20% of improved productivity available just by fixing that. People are working hard, but not in a Lean manner. This is what you will seek to change, and your business will perform better."

"I can't buy into a 20% productivity gain." Geoff seemed almost offended by the idea.

"This you can achieve and more. Your productivity will be gained not from what you see, but from what you do not see," Jorge added. "Let me explain."

With that, he moved to a whiteboard and began to draw a couple of pictures. "Your flow loss is coming from several problems. One is poor material supply. Not lack of sufficient material, but one of readily available material."

"Please, explain." Geoff was suddenly interested.

"By ready material, I am referring to the fact that you are committing material to products in a way that is not in the same sequence as the market is demanding. When the market demands something, you already have it made into something else and you must consider it no longer available. Inventory is building from materials that you cannot consume because you have already consumed their mating parts into other things that are also sitting in your finished goods because your customer does not need them. Thus, yes, you have sufficient material, but it is not ready."

"But we've processed it for another order?" asked Geoff.

"Not an order." Jorge paused. "You are using them for many of reasons. You want to use your machine capacity and your manpower resources efficiently, so you make things you can, but do not need.

"When you use up material to be efficient, but you do so on products that are not needed now or just to utilize human capacity, it is waste. This is because you are not actually making things to sell today. When you make products not being asked for, it is inefficient. It is even worse when you make products that are not in demand and you use valuable material that cannot be replaced until your suppliers can respond to do so. Just because you want to keep workers busy, you forfeit the ability to fill a different order for several more days or even weeks; whatever the supplier lead time is for those parts. Even so, the workers will come back tomorrow with possibly nothing to do. Both the workers' efforts and the materials consumed are misused. I will tell you that *it is impossible to be more efficient than demand will allow you to be*. You must gain your productivity from having the correct manpower to meet 'Takt' and then enabling them to do so."

Geoff sat very quietly for a moment before responding in an almost questioning tone. "But, with only sixteen weeks to deliver a product that takes twenty weeks to build, something has to be ready before an order is accepted in order to compress the lead time."

"I agree, but you have some options." Jorge smiled at Geoff. "Let me show you them. First, you must understand the normal takt and its variations for each of your products. I have calculated that you have enough machines to meet takt, so your challenge is to staff them properly. Your processing times are faster than takt, so moving your workforce through the processes will be a better strategy than to place people on all of them all of the time. Because of the high variety of products you make, you may never be able to optimize labor, which means your focus on productivity is really sub-optimization."

"Please allow me to provide another example." Jorge continued. "One of your products takes only 6 days to build, is that not correct? When I was looking at your management of that product, I discovered that you had over thirty days of orders out on your floor."

"That's because we offer that product on a thirty-day lead time." Dick offered.

"But you see, the orders are not being worked on in the way that you accepted them. They are being worked on based on something other than their due date. This is causing excess work in process and missed deliveries."

"How should we fix that?" asked Geoff.

"If your processing time is six days, then you must have no more than six days of orders on the floor. There may be times when you might need to level demand somewhat, but for now, limit the orders on the floor to match your thruput time of six days."

He went on to explain his recommended solutions in some detail, providing directional estimates for how much improvement opportunity might be available and his thoughts on how long it would take to achieve it. "Right now you have too many people and too many machines, you try to run them too fast, and the excess product clogs up your flow."

"I've been telling you that there were too many people for the work on the floor for a month, but you kept saying you couldn't get the work through!" Jolene sounded perturbed.

"This is the result of poor flow—lost labor. Before I leave, there is one more critical observation I would like to make," Jorge added. "Your paper processes do not flow at the same speed of the work as in the rest of the business and, therefore, they hold it back. This, too, you must correct. If you manufacture at takt, your papers must flow at takt as well!"

From there, he answered a few questions from the team and made a closing comment or two. As he began to pack for departure, I was compelled to approach him. "Jorge, I appreciate all of your comments, but I'm still not certain of exactly where to start."

"First find takt and flow production from the customer order point for each product," he responded abruptly as if I hadn't been listening. Nothing more was offered in response as he hoisted his bag headed to his rental car.

My staff and I met immediately afterward. "What do you suppose he meant by *that*?" I asked them.

Geoff spoke first. "I think he means we should start after assembly, which is really where the configuration point for most orders is established."

Karen, the plant controller, spoke next: "Well, we learned that we should start at the customer end of the process, so maybe what he was saying was that we should start where the product gets committed and then flow from there."

"Let's first do what he said and find takt for each product," I followed up. "From there we can use some standard hours reports and see just how far off we are from a manpower standpoint. Also, let's do a walk and see where our inventory is accumulating. I would guess that anything piled up after the configuration point is a bad thing."

"If all of our products are custom, isn't the configuration point where they first hit the floor?" Dick spoke up next.

"You must be looking to work in manufacturing, Dick. But the answer is, not really!" Geoff answered. "Several of our products have generic stages and others are actually re-configured on the shipping dock. We may be able to get their configuration points moved to a better point in the process."

After considerable discussion, we agreed that Jorge's message was to achieve flow from the point a product was committed to a customer or order, which actually varied by product. Karen's observation that we should start at the end of the process and work to achieve flow moving backward into the facility was exactly right. In contrast to a typical constraint-busting approach, flowing from order fulfillment at the customer's rate of demand would produce immediate improvements in response, reduce inventory, stabilize output, and make it more predictable. Treating each product individually would also provide a sequenced game plan for improvement. While chasing bottlenecks might provide for more dramatic, early improvements, it would also have the team scampering around processes in search of the next bottleneck. Since the net results are always dependent on the next constraint, the game plan would constantly be morphing itself. Worse yet, instead of turning the focus on the fulfillment of specific customer needs, we would instead be focused on the chase for process performance. It seemed like clearing the path starting at the end would work better for us in our present situation.

During the next several months, we employed some external guidance along with supplemental training to re-energize our Lean transformation. We tackled the entire fulfillment process, beginning with the highest impact products for specific customers. Our problems weren't the highest volume items, but rather some middle and low volume niche products with erratic order patterns that disrupted the operation. We separated the two order categories, and by working parallel paths for both high and low volume manufacturing flows, we elevated our performance at our main customer quickly enough for us to exit their performance improvement plan after only the first round of improvements. Further, our performance at all customers improved.

As the ninety-day deadline approached, it was time to call the staff together to prepare for the performance review that we had committed to.

"Well team, it would appear we have exceeded what they had required of us. Geoff, can you please give me your performance data for the customer review?"

"I sure can. First, I would like to thank every member of the team for their support and assistance in achieving these goals. Our number one problem of delivery to customer request has improved from about 51% to 80%. While that doesn't sound overwhelmingly impressive, please realize that we averaged three to four weeks late previously, and today we are at worst one to three days late. In every case when we are late, we are notifying them of the timetable and getting their agreement on those very slight reschedules."

"Do we understand what it will take to fix the one to three day problem?" Dick asked the question just a moment before I did.

"We do, and right now it's just getting the operations team to understand how to manage our manpower transitions in the new flow system. That, and we still have a couple of supplier lead time issues to tighten up. Janet does have them working well with us. I expect to be on time, all of the time, by the end of next month."

"What else can we talk about Geoff." I wanted us to keep moving.

"Well, the customers number two issue was their receiving quality, and the biggest problem there was actually missing parts in the parts kits. We actually took that to zero almost immediately through containment, and then worked with Johns team to develop a standard kit that applied to all of their orders, and then some supplemental kits for the rest. We turned those into visual checklists, cleaned up the standard work, and both the problem and the containment step are completely gone."

"Outstanding." I responded. "Dick, what kind of feedback are they giving you?"

"Once in while someone over there will say that we made it look so easy that they don't understand why it wasn't done earlier. But to be honest, they are simply blown away."

"What progress have we made on the support processes?" I looked to the rest of the team.

"As Geoff said, we have been able to work with some critical suppliers and shorten their response times with some minor inventory agreements." Janet added.

"And we have added a fast track to the more standard orders to get them through in a day, giving Janet more time to procure, and Geoff time to schedule better." John added.

"Great work to everyone. Let's schedule a celebration lunch for the entire organization. I want them to be aware of our progress, but also remind them we still have more work to do."

With that, we wrapped up our customer report-out and went back to work.

Our other products produced in those and similar value streams benefitted from the same improvements, helping us increase sales by nearly 15%, and increasing our profitability on those products eightfold, while our overall productivity improvements surpassed Jorge's prediction of twenty percent to thirty. This first really cohesive Lean implementation was a runaway success, a clear victory for everyone that also saved us from a possible business-altering change with a key customer.

Jorge was also correct to advise us to review and improve our paper processes at the same time. Several of them—purchasing approvals, accounts payable, and shipping—were found to be impacting floor performance and were completely reworked. They were no longer allowed to impose delays in manufacturing, and the addition of fast-track and problem escalation routes really helped with our manufacturing response times.

Typically associated with manufacturing, Lean principles actually apply to the improvement of any and every business activity conceivable. Techniques that originated around streamlining factory workflow have been transferred successfully into restaurants, retail stores, office environments, hospitals, and even construction and refinery sites. Lean's relentless focus on the elimination of waste through the creation of an efficient flow of value-added activities allows it to be applicable, often with immense impact, to any business.I don't consider myself a Lean expert, as that honor is reserved for those who think about it a lot more than I do. However, my own experience in Lean spans nearly thirty years of using the individual tools and another twenty of those developing my practitioner skills. During this time, my successes have enabled me to appreciate its power, as well as its difficulties in implementation. We're covering Lean at this point in the book for two reasons: first, the simplicity inherent to Lean solutions are fundamental to the charter of this book; second, as a career Lean practitioner, I'd like to try to simplify and promote its magic, while leaving most of the theoretical, technical, and tool details to others.

Lean Commandments

As a "hands-in" implementer of Lean, my belief is that there are just a few core "commandments" that cannot be ignored. Let's try to understand what they are, how they can help improve performance, and how failing to attend to them can impede progress.

1. **Start with the Customer:** The primary objective of your Lean effort is to become adaptive enough to respond to any level of market demand in the timeframe your customer or market wants it. Simply put, it means *becoming* the competitive benchmark! Consider your customer to be the "creator" of demand, and define him as anyone from a business patron to an associate sitting nearby who is the downstream user of your product or service (from material goods to data). What's imperative to understand about the customer relationship, beyond the type of products or services they buy or use, is the rate in which they consume them. In Lean speak, that rate of market demand is referred to as *takt*, and it's the fundamental building block for the design of all of the fulfillment processes for your goods or services *and* their supporting processes. Being certain you're structured to handle market and customer needs at the rate they are required is a key success factor, so we'll expand on *takt* shortly.

2. **Engage your people:** The second commandment is nearly as important as the first. The people in your organization already possess most of the skills and capability necessary to work through challenges and sustain or improve performance. But, because it requires their complete commitment, you must "manage to engage" your associates as a key success factor for leadership. Begin with the set of business-leading indicators you have already defined (markets, strategy, takt, economy), and

provide your associates with the information and direction that will motivate them to focus their efforts on improvement. Engagement that immerses them in the success of the business also gives them a personal stake. Lean is a heavily people-dependent set of processes where one of the most common failures is that of not engaging your team sufficiently.

A sizeable part of this book is devoted to the topic of engagement because it's so critical in its ability to involve those who are closest to the issues. The Lean tools will equip them with the skills to correct issues more effectively; engaging them harnesses the collective power of their intelligence and experience to achieve accelerated solutions. Their buy-in congeals into the glue of sustainability, but it always dissolves under inconsistent management actions that break down the fledgling disciplines before they can take root.

3. **Find your *takt* and use it:** Understanding demand in your own market (and its patterns, if any) is the most logical starting point to determine how to satisfy your customer's needs. While takt alone can give you a picture of overall customer demand, a conversion calculation to turn that demand into time or *"Takt Time"*, defines the amount of time you have to provide a single unit of product or service event to keep pace with the rate of demand. The formula is a simple one:

$$Takt\text{-}time = demand\ /\ time\ available$$

A quick note to this formula: "demand" is the known market requirement for your product or service, and "time available" is a conversion of the resources you have to fulfill your share of market demand, into time. You may choose to level, average, or share-factor demand in order to develop the most usable picture of any market. "Time available" can be based upon a person, a machine or group of machines, a function, a department, or even an entire office complex, factory, or factories that supply the specific product or service. A simple example of *takt time* is the requirement to ship one unit or perform one service during every minute of operation. I want to emphasize that although the usual interpretation of *takt* refers to pieces or units of output, we shouldn't limit ourselves to that definition. Substituting activities (for instance, customer service opportunities per hour, patient arrivals, etc.) in lieu of units of output is the best way to apply it to non-manufacturing applications.

Although the calculation of *takt* can become challenging when you're trying to combine different markets, products, and/or service offerings, the conversion to *takt time*, can almost get contentious. In practice it becomes very easy to confuse *takt-time* with process time or cycle time (the time that the *process takes* to complete a unit or service) and it's important to keep a laser focus on the difference, because it's the process that has to be converted to fulfill market demand at the pace of that demand. The impact of variable demand on *takt-times* can be further complicated by diverse fulfillment processes that employ equally variable resources: equipment, disparate parts of the organization, even different sources of supply. Multiple departments in an organization might sometimes compete for control of specific elements of the fulfillment processes, making them even less predictable. Fractioned response systems might have several response cycles that cumulatively result in sub-optimized systems. It takes a homogenized version of *takt/takt-time* to determine the response cycles for the entire organization, as well as the proper resources to ensure it remains Lean throughout. Remember that the basic purpose of *takt time* is to convert demand into resource time so that units of output can be measured against the resource inputs. Every one of your fulfillment and support processes must be structured to perform at the rate of overall *takt* (within takt time), and it takes discipline of leadership to focus your organization on the simplest yet most effective method.

4. **Seek "Flow":** The objective of the Lean tools is to achieve a smooth flow of the activities necessary to deliver your product or services at the rate your customers demand them (*takt*) with minimal waste. That's a mouthful, and it's far harder to achieve than it sounds. If every segment of your fulfillment processes performs at *takt* and is supported at *takt*, the response cycles should connect to yield continuous flow. I'll emphasize the word "supported" to stress that fulfillment processes that are able to flow at *takt* are quite frequently constrained by the administrative processes that surround them. That's why it's essential to build the same response capability into them in order to enable the rest of the organization to achieve its demand response goal. Failure to do so will result in rework activities throughout the organization, disconnected flow, added cost, and dulled response. To accomplish this, you'll need to use *takt* as the basis to reconstruct your fulfillment processes with a focus on process simplification, alignment to *takt-time*, and inter-connections that will establish and sustain an operating rhythm that supports its attainment.

Achieve Flow

With *takt* defined, you'll next have to determine your ability to deliver those products or services within *takt-time*. I'll refer to this as "***Thruput***," which is a common, but not universal, term used to define the current response capability of your fulfillment processes. Thruput-time is the conversion of your delivery system to a time metric. It's different than *takt-time* in that it focuses on the aggregated total time required for a product or service to take shape through your process(es) before it can end up in the hands of a satisfied customer (for example, three days of thruput time, with 1 unit completing every minute at takt time). The *takt-time* in a service business could require that you process one person through a waiting line every five minutes, even though the total time your customers invest in you from the moment they call or enter your waiting line to the point you complete their requests for services might be a half hour. In manufacturing, thruput can represent the total time required to bring a product from raw material to shipment. Thruput-time has two components: 1) Processing or Cycle Time; and 2) Movement or Waiting time.

As you begin your Lean effort, it's necessary for you to understand thruput-time and its breakdown in order to calculate your ability to improve response. As you do, it will not be uncommon to find movement/waiting time much larger than process or cycle time. Though both can be improved, focusing first on non-process time can usually provide greater gains faster, and for less cost and effort. You can find thruput time by adding cycle (process) times and inventory cues (measured in hours or days of usage), using a stopwatch to measure it directly (like a service), or simply by attaching a tag to a representative product and asking each person who touches it to check it in and out. Exercises of this type are helpful to understand and address your response time capability.

Processing time is usually viewed as value-added (not waste), whereas movement and waiting will take the form of either non-value-added time (waste) or necessary non-value-added (unavoidable waste). The Lean objective is to build systems that guarantee continuous flow from the start of the process to its finish. Improving that flow involves separating waste from the value-added activities in each process step and eliminating it. From there you can more easily streamline the value-added work, enabling greater efficiency and faster thruput, while preserving the critical customer deliverables.

Pitch - Alternatively, there is yet another aspect to the thruput/response equation that can be useful as an aid in executing fulfillment. It is referred to as **Pitch**, and while it's used differently by various Lean practitioners, I prefer to use it to describe an increment of flow that is established by either the business or the marketplace.

A real-life example of pitch might be a dozen eggs, which is equal to a pitch of 12. I'll offer no research into why eggs are predominantly packaged in dozens; chickens certainly don't lay them 12 at a time! But the dozen egg carton is the predominant method of offering them to the market. Although pitch can be a derivative of the method of transportation, with eggs it's more likely evolved either by habit or tradition. Because a dozen eggs is so entrenched in the way the market buys them, the effort to change market pitch could be more difficult and costlier than might be any gains from doing so.

Another, more definable manufacturing example of pitch might be socks. Because of their use in pairs, socks are sold in pairs. It's unlikely they are produced in pairs, but they may be made in larger batches that are divisible by two (that would be a pitch of 2 applied to a batch size). Other products that are sold in pairs as both right- and left-hand versions also have to be matched, such as gloves and shoes, so in these examples, pitch is a necessary tool to simplify flow through the manufacturing, packaging, and distribution processes. There are many other examples of pitch where the multiples driven by consumption should be integrated into the fulfillment processes. Pitch is an aspect of demand or flow that is important, because ignoring it can result in waste, and leveraging it has the power to reduce costs.

Avoid Sub-optimization

Practicing Lean necessitates an awareness of the concept of sub-optimization. This occurs when you increase performance within a segment or subset of a process, but do not improve the output of the production or service system, thereby failing to obtain an overall benefit. Both factory and business processes suffer from sub-optimization, and it's usually self-inflicted. I've seen many organizations invest capital in additional machines and office equipment to improve the thruput of a part of their process only to ignore or merely relocate the real problem and gain far less than the value of the investment.

One example of sub-optimization can be found at a retail store where the staffing is perfectly resourced to assist customers with their selection or to replenish purchased products on the shelves, but lacks an adequate number of store associates with cashier skills. This might leave customers standing in line and frustrated, or even abandoning their purchases. The reverse is also possible, where cashiers are standing at their stations waiting for customers, but there is no one to assist with product selection. This problem is easily solved by cross training, a training matrix, and monitoring cues.

Avoiding sub-optimization requires discipline, preparation, and a thorough understanding of your entire process or system. It also necessitates a clear picture of the demand that flows through the process and alignment of the resources available to fulfill that demand.

When I stress that your administrative processes should be aligned to have the same response capability as your "physical" or delivery processes, my favorite example is order entry. I've seen countless examples where the activities around order receipt and processing consume far more than their fair share of the lead time available to create and deliver the goods or services, making on-time fulfillment less likely. Another example comes from operations planning, where a business plan developed to fulfill a specific level of market demand becomes disheveled by fluctuations in market activity, stressing the organization's internal and external resources. This variation creates imbalances that move back and forth from materials supply to the fulfillment processes and back into demand planning, disrupting the entire system. Solutions that are deployed in an un-level or untimely fashion to only a few of these inputs rather than all of them will create sub-optimized performance that always has repercussions for both cost and revenue.

The concept of sub-optimization requires that you always maintain a "system-level view" of your improvement efforts, identifying flow and performance improvements that will have the greatest, most direct impact on your ability to improve response time for the entire system. Projects that cannot be leveraged to have a system impact should be delayed until they do, or eliminated entirely.

Manage the Use of Cycles of Response

Having covered the Lean Commandments, it's time to introduce another key success factor for the deployment of Lean. The creation of a continuous flow of process activities requires all systems to move in harmony with one another, and this timing must be replicated throughout all of the business functions. I'll refer to these as "cycles of response" because of the way they can synchronize all business activities to align with the *takt-time* for the business. In a manufacturing environment, successful response to changes in customer demand is the cumulative product of aligning four primary response cycles: a) on your supply chain (material goods or services), b) your internal fulfillment processes, c) a management cycle to align the administrative processes, and d) a customer cycle that represents the time between their request for goods or services and the expected delivery of them. Aligning each of these to a version of *takt-time* is an aspect that is too often overlooked in many Lean implementations.

Let's start by identifying the response cycles that cannot be changed directly—the ones *we* must align *to* because we don't have the power to entirely align them to ourselves. The most important of these is the time the market allows for delivery of products or services in response to a request, without losing customers or impeding market growth. Often called "Lead Time," this should usually be determined by your competitive environment. "Market-defined" means you have to align to it, and you can't change it without redefining the requirement by developing a product or process that's so compelling people will wait for it, or by developing response capabilities that exceed those of the competition, thereby reducing lead time for the market and gaining a competitive advantage. Another way to gain advantage is by subdividing your market response offerings, such as faster response times for higher volume or competitive offerings and slower response times on low volume or custom offerings. Dependability of performance is a huge response advantage—the more customers *can* rely on you—the more they will do so! How innovative you are in building your market response-model can become a game-changer that leads you to success, but without the ability to make improvements like those, you'll have to align with the rest of the market or risk losing share.

The second cycle that also can't be changed (although we have more influence in this case) is the time it takes for suppliers of the products and services used by our business to respond to generate *our* own products and services. Good management practices, such as the placement of strategic inventory, dual capacity models, or supply agreements that cover lead time for different business levels such as volume and mix changes, can facilitate response during times of market instability. Still, it's constructive to understand that you don't have absolute control over it.

These two cycles establish the bookends for the design of your own response systems. The open challenge is for you to construct your internal systems, both demand fulfillment as well as management processes, to be as robust and quickly adaptable to changes in the market as possible, so they can compensate for disruptions in the two external cycles. Great system designs will blend internal management controls, processing requirements, capacity, and investment (people, equipment, inventory, and facilities) into a usable formula that will allows you to adjust to changes in market *takt* fluidly, and inside of that market's lead time. If you can't adjust capacity to match changes in demand, you will either turn business away or spend yourself into a less profitable position trying to fulfill it.

Active adjustments to market changes are more readily done in organizations that manage highly developed forecasts for demand, supply, and capacity consumption. In a Lean environment, you define your market *takt,* then structure your delivery processes—for services or hard goods—with the appropriate facilities, equipment, and staffing to enable you to meet *takt-time.* Once accomplished, your ability to respond is then limited to your least adaptable process, otherwise known as constraint management.

There are some key differences between office processes and service or manufacturing ones. For office and (sometimes for) service processes, *takt-time* can be difficult to determine. Both can lack a defined scope of work and measured process thruput times that will prevent you from calculating time available, thus aligning them to *takt* can take considerable effort. Also, because the staffing decisions for these processes tend to be based on "positions" that don't actually have measured work, staffing levels become "fixed" and are less able to flex tasks, index performance, or adjust to changes in demand unless someone with sufficient experience intervenes. Many businesses are constrained by the performance of their administrative processes, causing uneven demand responses that are rarely mitigated. The effects often degrade the performance of the fulfillment processes in a way that is less visible.

Matching the performance cycles of administrative processes to those of your fulfillment processes *will* improve the performance of your business. If an abnormality in a fulfillment process requires a corrective response (an example might be an emergency purchase), then your approval and processing steps to procure the item must be able to respond in the same cycle time as the need. By understanding and converting the administrative workflows to flex with takt time, you can establish a response capability for your business processes that's in sync with the market needs.

In building business-wide cycles of response, start by identifying the key processes across the entire business that can affect its performance. From there, you can prioritize by a process's importance to your delivery processes, align their capabilities, and determine the level of resources they will need to sustain a timely response. When we get to metrics in Chapter eight, these cycles of response will be extended into your review and feedback activities, which should facilitate your ability to generate timely corrective action and implement process improvement.

Using the Lean Tools

In the 1999 Harvard Business Review article, "Decoding the DNA of the Toyota Production System[1]," the authors highlighted four key attributes of Lean that should serve as the pillars of your own response processes. They are paraphrased below:

1. All work is highly specified for content, sequence, timing, and outcome.

2. Every customer to supplier connection is direct.

3. The pathway for delivery of each product or service is simple.

4. Improvement methods are logical, mentored, and performed at the lowest level.

Each of these themes requires a separate focus and integrated effort in order to achieve true Lean results and commensurate success. To achieve these goals, I've dindividual Lean

LEAP Tool Set	Objective	Lean Tools	Process
FLOW	1. Connect Customers to Suppliers 2. Simplify the Product Path 3. Deliver to the Customer on their terms	Value Stream Mapping/Takt Continuous Flow Pull Systems	Key Elements to Flow the Value Stream
STANDARD WORK	1. Work content, Sequence and Timing are highly specified 2. The Value Stream is continuously improving 3. Cost objectives are attained	5s Standard Work Setup Reduction TPM	1) Translate Takt 2) Major Step 3)Key Points 4) Reason Why
JIDOKA	1. Improvement techniques are logical, performed at the lowest level, and mentored 2. The Value Stream is self correcting 3. Quality exceeds the Customers expectations	Visual Management Autonomation Error Proofing	Establish the Value Stream visually - use the other tools to contain and sustain
CONTINUOUS IMPROVEMENT	1. Promote associate Safety and development 2. Evolve to a Lean Culture	Employee engagement & training Business Metrics	Combined use of the tools to engage the workforce and build a continuous improvement mindset

---

[1] Decoding the DNA of the Toyota Production System C1999 by Harvard Business Review - S.Spear and H.K.Bowen

Each tool group contains the individual Lean tools that interrelate and have implementation synergies. I'm not planning to go all the way into the detailed tools in this book, however, you can find more on the interrelationships in the addendum. My purpose here, is to provide insight about the main themes, why they exist, how they relate, and how to simplify their use and avoid complexity.

The Flow Tools: R=A+D

Lean Tool Group	Result	Approach (Tools)	Deployment (Process)
Flow	Connect customers and suppliers	Value stream mapping / *takt*	5 Value Stream design elements: *takt*, activity flow, inventory, process design, customer order point
	Simplify the product / service path	Continuous flow	
	Deliver to the customer	Pull Systems	

Flow Tools

This group includes Value Stream Mapping (VSM), continuous flow processing and pull systems. They are coupled for their collective ability to identify and facilitate the flow of activities. Used as the primary planning tool for a Lean effort, value stream or process mapping begins with *takt* and collects all of the process data required to enable you to understand and expose the inner workings of a value stream. Populated with the correct data, the map serves as a structured planning tool by which you can establish improvement priorities.

A thoroughly prepared map helps to identify opportunities for flow improvement and is also helpful in selecting projects that use the other Lean tools to facilitate linkage into a continuous flow of activities. Fulfilling customer needs through the use of pull system buffers and triggers allows the system to respond fluidly to changes in demand and assists you in establishing predictable performance. Lean approaches further minimize investment in assets, inventory, and manpower.

The flow tools work in unison to focus your efforts on process sequencing and waste elimination, shortening processing time and reducing your cost for products and services without losing business due to forsaken demand.

Standard Work Tools: R=A+D

Lean Tool Group	Result	Approach (Tools)	Deployment (Process)
Standard Work	Work content and sequence is highly specified	5s / Standard work	1)Define *takt* 2)Major step 3)Key points 4)Reason why Integrate the Lean Tools
	The value stream is continuously improving	Standard work	
	Cost objectives are obtained	Total Productive Maintenance (TPM)	

Standardized Work

One of Lean's most powerful and broadly applicable concepts is standardized work. Although we've already touched upon it on several occasions, it's difficult to adequately underscore its importance. The essence of standard work is simplicity, with its greatest value being in its contribution of repeatability, discipline, and predictable performance.

How is it simple? First, for the work in question, standard work is highly focused, asking only, "What is the major task to be completed?" In other words, what segment of the product and service delivery process am I working on here? The "Major Step" describes the primary objective of the process work sequence. It might represent a single assembly operation, processing a bill for payment, or even taking a patient's blood pressure and pulse as a function of a pre-checkup routine. Next, standard work asks, "What are the Key Points?" Again, focusing on the specific process step, these are items to be monitored or watched by the person(s) executing the process. Key points can include maintaining critical quality or product features—assuring incoming quality for the next process down the line, or possibly the act of completing a checklist for the client in question.

The final element in standard work involves the question, "What's the Reason Why?" Providing associates with meaning for their task steps and process verifications goes a long way toward ensuring they will consistently perform in line with the instructions. While it may sound prescriptive, the intent of the major step is to clearly identify the work elements to be completed, in line with the key points, to insure a consistent result, always reinforced by the reasons why. Together they collaboratively insure that associates don't introduce randomness to the process that might jeopardize the desired result. In the construction of standard work, each question should be answered simply but completely, with the three elements forming the "standard" for the "work" to be completed.

The Lean tools that make up the Standardized Work group were selected for their ability to contribute to a more complete result. They include 5s (workplace cleanliness and organization), Standard Work (detailed process work scope), Total Productive Maintenance (operator sustained equipment conditions), and Setup Reduction (streamlining process changeovers). Elements of each of these tools should be combined as applicable into a master "Standard Work" document for a given process. Although certain elements of standard work will originate from various areas of the business (examples include engineering specifications and customer quality requirements), the best approach is to have the associates who actually perform the work write-up as much of the process as possible. Not only will the instructions be more accurate and user-friendly, but the associate involvement in its development also will motivate them to pursue the most efficient processing options, keep their work areas in order, and monitor or maintain the performance of equipment they are assigned to.

Jidoka: R=A+D			
Lean Tool Group	Result	Approach (Tools)	Deployment
Jidoka	Improvement methods are logical, mentored, and at the	Visual Management	Establish the value stream visually – use the other tools to steer Associate behaviors to contain, correct, improve, and sustain
	The value Stream is self-correcting	Autonomation	
	Quality is provided in the eyes of the customer	Six-sigma	

Jidoka: Problem Resolution Tools

"Jidoka" is a word sometimes used to refer to a group of tools and a system that helps associates identify the causes of abnormal performance, as well as providing the appropriate responses for problems that will prevent or correct them in the future. In combination, the tools I group under Jidoka provide associates with the skills to self-monitor and diagnose their processes, empowering them to improve those processes using documented Standard Work as their baseline. This is a very powerful group of Lean tools that are too often overlooked or undervalued because of the difficulty in implementation and the discipline required to sustain them. Jidoka is extremely valuable for its ability to instill operational discipline, creating the momentum for continuous improvement through engagement and significantly improving sustainability.

I group three lean tools under Jidoka: Error Proofing (the use of process-based and logical problem-solving tools to eliminate the ability to create a defective product or service), Visual Management (visual tools and systems that can immediately communicate the status of the workplace and request action), and Autonomation (the analysis of the interaction between operators and process-based equipment to maximize the effectiveness of both).

Used in concert with "Behavioral Pull" techniques, Jidoka tools can fundamentally transform your culture's ability to respond to problems, correct or elevate a request for assistance, sustain the solutions, and enable consistent customer response. Thorough deployment of Jidoka can result in an environment that self-corrects itself to become progressively more responsive to minor deviations in operational performance, thereby driving sustainment.

Continuous Improvement: R=A+D

Lean Tool Group	Result	Approach (Tools)	Deployment (Process)
Continuous Improvement	Prioritize employee safety and Wellness as number one	Value stream Mapping	Combined use of the tools to train, engage, and build a continuous improvement mindset
	Evolve to a Lean culture	Associate engagement, Feedback and Improve Loop	

Continuous Improvement

The last of my thematic grouping of Lean tools covers the development of behaviors and skills that will sustain your gains and drive additional improvements. Setting the stage for continuous improvement involves building a consistent group of management behaviors that we'll simplistically refer to as "management commitment." This commitment consists of an implementation plan for comprehensive employee training and involvement which will develop an associate's Lean skills while also building critical energy for achieving their engagement. Also included under continuous improvement is a layered auditing program (Chapter eight) to monitor and encourage compliance. Finally, it requires a set of metrics to monitor and guide your program that are explainable, and are understood to be applicable for all levels of the organization. The concept of continuous improvement implies that there is also a methodology for converting the newly attained benchmarks, and the lessons learned during their achievement, into an evolutionary process that creates a "feedback loop" to accelerate improvement even more. These steps serve as the "cement" that will sustain and support carry-forward gains.

Implementing Lean

Not every Lean tool will be required in all environments, but there is a dependent relationship among many of them, and a well-executed Lean program will use one or more of the tools and techniques under each of the four themes. Said differently, you should use the tools that will enable all activities to flow in as standardized a process as possible, with a clean, visual, responsive environment that engages associates in such a way that enables them to diagnose and correct problems so rapidly that continuously improvement becomes commonplace. Again, for more on the Lean Tools and their relationships, see the tables in the addendum.

So, how can you make something as simple as this so difficult to implement? There are many ways to fail with Lean. You can overuse or underuse the tools, complicate the transformation with restrictions or unreasonable goals, or interject activities out of priority, slowing implementation. Management must adjust its own behaviors, taking care not to impose expectations or constraints that will diffuse engagement, while fully supporting the implementation and empowering associates through a paced deployment of the necessary skills. The rate of implementation should ensure that all of the dependent tools are implemented in support of one another and not individually. Even when results are impressive and momentum builds, impatience cannot be allowed to radically alter a plan that is working properly at other levels. Finally, attempting to move too quickly (outpacing the rate of learning with a compressed implementation sequence) will cause you to leave people behind, curtailing full engagement.

It became clear to me early in my own Lean journey that an implementation is incredibly counterintuitive, and each year that fact becomes more apparent. Once you learn to cast aside performance metrics achieved with sub-optimized value streams in favor of the more cohesive performance of an optimized, *flowing* value stream, the benefits will be far greater. A number of years ago, I allowed an improvement team to re-flow a machining cell improperly, just because they needed learn more about the actual improvement methods themselves. While the lesson had a negative cost impact in the short term, its engagement value was a real bargain. Once they discovered their solution wouldn't achieve the goal, the team quickly reconvened and committed to correct the problem, eventually driving more than 25% of the labor out of the cell and reducing the overall processing time by about 30%, benefits that far exceeded the cost of their "lesson." As an added benefit, future improvement efforts that involved members of the same team were even more beneficial, because they understood that their contribution would not be overridden. The lesson for my staff and I was that imposing restrictions on their ability to fail would truly have been sub-optimization.

Providing a product or service to market is easier, more predictable, and more efficient when you use the correct Lean tools with the right plan. Attempting to do it without enough tools can yield sub-optimized business performance.

"Measure only what you can act upon, and no more. When you measure, make sure that the meaning of the metric is understood by the entire organization."

Jorge's words still make complete sense, years later.

Developing a set of metrics that will consistently direct your business in good times and bad, and whose meanings can be understood by the organization, is an essential management skill. One of the potential causes of a failed Lean program is the tendency to focus on poorly defined, excessive, or incorrect metrics, clinging to them by tradition rather than functionality. Chapter eight will help you to simplify the metrics challenge.

Chapter 8: The ABC's of SQDC+T

Simplified Metrics that Self-Improve

1. The Motive to Measure

2. Metric Types

3. Selecting Your Metrics

During the course of our efforts to streamline paper processes and improve customer service performance, we unearthed a number of disconnects in the definition and management of several key metrics that also impacted some lower level ones. These issues were masking our true performance for our customers, which was far worse than what we were actually seeing internally. With this discovery propelling us, we revisited our business objectives to clarify exactly what performance indicators we should be measuring and how they should be measured. We would then have to determine how to implement the changes, communicate them, deploy them, and monitor them effectively.

"Well, after a deep dive into our issues at all customers, it's become clear to me that we're measuring so many things in this business that we've lost focus on tracking the indicators that matter," I started. "Further, we aren't always taking action on what we measure, which is the first clue that we may not need to measure it."

"Can you give us an example?" Karen asked.

"For one, we measure factory performance from about eight different angles, and the results actually contradict themselves in a couple of cases. Only two of these metrics are really essential to the health of the business. Let's review the metrics we're tracking in the business today as a team."

I slid a pair of packets across the table to each of my staff. The top one was a list of every current metric and their trends, about 30-ish in all. Underneath the cover list was a thin packet of six sheets with only headings.

"When we look at how we measure our business, we should try to see it from multiple perspectives. First, should be our customers, using our business metrics to understand how we should reflect their needs and their expectations of us. Next, we should consider our internal stakeholders, both owners and associates. How do our metrics reflect their needs? Are they clear enough for them to understand their role in achieving our goals? Finally, we need to consider the needs of the business itself, because if our metrics don't protect its needs, everybody loses.

"To answer some of those questions and to keep our top-level metrics as simple as possible, I'm going to introduce to you a formula: $SQDC^2+T$. There is one page for each of these letters in your packets and our objective for today is to come up with our own definition of each. I like to call these our 'Public' metrics because they will be publicized to everyone in the business.

"Please just flip the list of current metrics over and let's start with the second page titled 'Safety/Wellness.' Even though the customer is technically always first, we'll always start with Safety, so let's see if we can identify the key measurement for our business in this category."

"Well, it's obviously factory safety," Geoff said.

"Is it?" I challenged. "Is factory safety alone really inclusive enough for the entire organization?"

"It does cover the greater part of the employee population," Mary said. "But maybe, to your question, it's possibly a feeder metric to a broader wellness goal."

"It's a valid point and one we should decide on as a team based upon our best knowledge of the business." I was, again, coaching. "As always, let's make sure we take both an external and an internal view for each metric."

"How do we view safety externally?" John sounded puzzled.

"Are our products safe enough? Is there a sub-metric for safety that supports an objective to have the safest products on the market? Do our packaging methods pose any risk to our customers or the environment?" I asked. "What about our public image? Are there things we can do as a major local employer to make our community safer?"

"I see." Maria said. "But doesn't a list like that just open us up to more measurements of things that we really can't influence?"

"Not if we don't let it. It's our choice."

With that, the team began to look at the metrics list and brainstorm ways to revise its structure.

The Safety discussion was the most interesting, primarily because the external view offered us many different options.

"What if our key Safety metric is rebuilt to include our entire associate group, as well as what we think of our products?" Janet asked.

"I would really like an outreach component, even if it's as simple as a weekly home safety theme that we publish in the newsletter. Let's make our people realize that we not only want them to work safely, but we want them to go home and return the next day, just as safely. It's also a subtle way of getting safety into their heads on a moment by moment basis" I added.

The team finally agreed to a four-walls safety metric that not only included the factory and office employees, but also covered any visitors to our facility. Once they had arrived at a top-level metric (triangulated between people, products and community) we wrote a one-page definition to clearly define its measurement logic. From there, we identified the lower level metrics for each subcategory that would feed that key metric, identified the staff champion, the reporting responsibilities, and the role each department would have in the achievement of the target.

"You've done a great job of looking externally for our Safety metric and more fully encompass the business challenges we're facing. From here we need to move on to the customer and turn all of our key metrics to look outward before we bring them inward with sub-metrics, just as we did with Safety. The next metric is customer quality. When we say the measure needs to focus outward, we're again referring to finding an external basis for establishing its goal. They should be defined and measured from the customer or stakeholder's perspective."

"So, you mean like the objectives set for us by the corporation?" Janet asked.

"Not entirely. The objectives set by the corporation are derived from an incremental improvement target over the prior year's baseline performance. When I say look outward, I want us to triangulate an objective from what our customer expects, what we know about the competitors in our market, and what we think our current capability is. If we just look internally or incrementally, we run the risk of not being competitive. If we triangulate correctly, it might lead us to a goal that will give us breakthrough performance."

"What if we really don't know all of that information?" Dick was thinking from a highly data-driven perspective.

"Then we'll lean toward what we know about our customers' objectives for us."

"If we simply focus on what the customer is seeing in their four walls or in the market, we won't be working on the right things internally." John was referring to the differences between defects at the customer, and those in the factory.

"With the kind of products we make, the two may never correlate. They will see usage failures that we will never see. But we should be using those to drive improvement on our end also." I answered

We repeated the process used for safety by reviewing the key metric definitions for their ability to fulfill the measurement intent. There were no problems with the customer quality metric, as it appeared to have a straightforward definition and an execution path that was representative of the correct intent. When we dug into the internal sub-level metrics, however, we confirmed that our operational metrics didn't necessarily align with what the customer was seeing, and we took steps to tighten the relationships.

Next, we moved to Customer Delivery, or Responsiveness. As we dug in, it became apparent that we'd been measuring entirely against our own internal criteria rather than the customer's. This played a large part in our failure to understand the severity of our performance issues.

"How do we measure delivery performance with the customer?" I asked, although I already knew the answer.

"We measure it against the delivery commitment we make as we accept the order." Geoff and Dick said in harmony.

"Is it the date they want, or one we assign?"

"It can be either, but most of the time it's one we assign based on our estimate of our lead time." Geoff said.

"In my mind, that's an internal metric. It's probably one we should keep, but I'd ultimately like to know if we are capable of responding in a way that's competitive to the market. In other words, responsiveness to their request rather than our capability." I pressed on.

"We came to this method because each of our customers was imposing different delivery requirements and evaluating us against their specific requirements. It made an overall metric too difficult to construct." Dick responded.

"My impression is that the basis for our metric should be their need-by date, even if it's outside of our ability to respond. It seems that's the best way of understanding what the market expects and whether or not we have a gap. We can also measure against our commitment as a sub-metric though."

The proposed change drew considerable grumbling, with both the sales and operations managers feeling that it wouldn't be useful. After some considerable discussion, we were finally able to modify a collective metric that could gauge our response to their requirements, but maintain a measure of performance against our own commitments. We continued this process placing definitions around two metrics for cost performance: one for product selling price and another for operational cost performance.

"Now let's look at the final metric category of Time!" I instructed. "When I say time, I'm thinking of our own market responsiveness."

"But I thought delivery was responsiveness," Dick said in a questioning tone.

"Nope, in this case we need to define a time-based objective for every organizational function that aligns with the market response time requirement. Some examples: In one organization, the financial team set a goal to be able to close the books in four days while actually achieving it in two! In an automotive business, the development teams could regenerate product every four to six years, but needed three. Since we, as a manufacturing organization, must perform at "Takt" each of our administrative and support functions should have a time-based objective that aligns with takt-time at the top level and then deploys to a sub-level metric within each function. The end goal is to comprehensively manage time in such a way that we make ourselves the leader in market response"

"How would we do that? I can't think of a measurement that would be any different than the one we built to perform to the customer request." Dick sounded dismayed.

"It would seem that we should base our responsiveness around the market benchmarks we have, if any. From there we can see if we are in position to reset it. Think in terms of Amazon. They have established the benchmark for consumer product delivery. Before that, Dell did it in computers. Neither played by the rules, but both redefined the expectations for response in their respective markets."

After extensive discussion, we agreed to a business responsiveness metric that was an incremental improvement over our own thruput time after we researched various competitive benchmarks and then developed a strategy to "one-up" our competitors.

By the end of the session we covered everything from safety to cost and from receipt of order to delivery of product right to the customer site. Each function had defined their contributing role in the improvement process. Most importantly, everyone in the organization would be engaged in some way to achieve the goal of best-in-class response to all of our customers.

"These key metrics will be used to drive our activities and enable our business to thrive. We'll communicate them to all associates and train everyone in both their meaning and measurement. Please realize that these aren't all of the things we'll need to measure in the business, but they are all we'll talk about and report on publicly. Whenever a metric slips off track, we'll drop down one pareto level at a time until we find the cause. Then we'll elevate our attention to that problem until the metric returns to normal and the performance problem disappears. Communication of these metrics will extend organization wide to enable everyone to clearly understand their meaning. Our commitment as leaders is to deploy resources that can actively resolve those problems within the timing needed."

I closed by clarifying the imperative behind the metrics program. "As the senior leadership team, our job is to help deploy the metrics across the entire organization by participating in workforce reviews and constantly asking individual associates whether they understand a given metric well enough to explain how they can personally impact its performance."

A number of years ago, during an interview for a very senior operations position with a company, I asked the hiring executive what he measured in his business. He proudly handed me a metrics package that was roughly 100-pages in length. Flipping through it quickly, I cautiously asked how many of those metrics he and his leadership team were truly able to take action on. When he responded, "All of them," it was clear to me that the job he had was of no interest to me. I'd already learned the hard way that no organization could properly focus on, or work-to-ground, that many metrics.

There are a great many organizations that over-measure their businesses. To use a common manufacturing example, they will measure headcount, labor efficiency, labor input, direct staff versus indirect staff, indirect labor efficiency, productivity, and salaried personnel. Unfortunately, the only meaningful measurement is how many people are required to provide the portfolio of services or products offered at the pace of market demand. Although they are actively measuring every individual in the building from four different angles, the common failure to perform the due diligence to understand exactly how the presence of each individual or role contributes to the value add to the business is often the missing element. In Lean, we refer to this as making wasteful activities more efficient; yet, no matter how efficient you can make them, in the end they are still waste.

A smaller number of companies tend to tie their evaluation of business performance to only one or two metrics. Whether the metric is financial or customer-based, a singular focus on one bell-weather metric ignores the fact that the dynamics in any business system will limit the perspective of any single metric to a narrow, one-dimensional view. A sound metric system uses multiple metrics with defined interrelationships to provide a three-dimensional view of performance.

Keeping your key metrics to a critical few measurements doesn't mean you don't measure other things; it just means that all of the things you do measure don't need to be positioned on your dashboard. The most important reason we limit the number of key metrics to a critical few is to promote broad organizational focus. Properly chosen, four to six key metrics reside at the top, and are fed from below by lower level or pareto metrics to drive the performance of the business. The objective is to make your status and progress toward your goals easier for everyone to understand and agree to.

Why Measure

Let's return to R=A+D and chapter three for just a moment. At the time, it was advised that you should first ask, "What *result* do I want" from a new strategy or initiative? Of course, the answer to that may come from somewhere other than yourself: your customer, your markets, your corporate headquarters, or possibly even from your own workforce. Once you answer that question, though, it might quickly lead you to determining the *approach* you should take in order to achieve that result, and also who you will need to *deploy* it to in order to achieve success. The initial act of defining the targeted result is the biggest step in setting the framework for what to measure through the course of your strategy.

Very often, a new strategy alone won't create a need for new metrics, but it will very likely establish different expectations for the existing ones in order to fully support the new business objectives. The changes may include modifications to their definitions, as it isn't unusual for traditional metrics to evolve over the life of a business in response to changes in its day-to-day needs. While they usually seem to align with true needs of the business, they are often modified by corrective actions that are imposed to address temporary business issues. Established metrics should perform the following functions: satisfy your stakeholder and market requirements, be meaningful to everyone in the organization, have concise definitions that can be clearly communicated, and be broadly and understood deployed. If they don't meet those requirements, it's time to push reset.

Structured as above, your metrics will have the best chance of being universally understood by all stakeholders, a necessity for driving behaviors that will support achievement of the business objectives, which is the real reason for measuring anyway.

Metric Types

If you asked 100 businesses to list their entire set of metrics, you might be astounded by both the size of list and the variation those lists would contain. Some of those metrics will tend to be similar among competitive business types whether they be financial businesses, marketing businesses, distribution operations, real estate sales offices, or manufacturing entities. Each will have a different group of unique and critical metrics, with indigenous definitions, yet they should broadly include the following:

1. Safety or Wellness: Employee-focused

2. Quality (of goods or services): Customer-focused (external customer "touching" first, internal process-focused at the second level)

3. Delivery (of goods or services): Customer-focused (delivery of products and services to customer needs measured against market-defined timing)

4. Cost: Externally focused (sales cost of delivering products and services against competitive market benchmarks)

5. Cost: Internally focused (cost of operating performance)

6. Time (a time-based response metric that is market supported and can be applied enterprise-wide

All of the above metrics are recommended as "Key" or "Global," top-level measurements that are placed in view of the entire organization for the purposes of communicating progress and soliciting action-based behaviors. It's normal and necessary to break these down into what I'll refer to as "sub-level" or "pareto" metrics, which drop down one level at a time and "feed" data upward to support the performance of the global metrics. These sub-level metrics provide a pathway to assist in determining the root causes of performance issues and guide the selection of corrective actions.

For the most part, your global metrics are results-based, or rear-facing. Again, these metrics are fed by sub-level metrics and serve both as diagnostics for problem resolution and as benchmarks to steer performance. The larger group of sub-level metrics breaks down into three categories, with the key separator being time—the amount of time it takes to review them and the time in which a corrective response is expected to be initiated. Let's look at each of the three groups.

Results metrics

The time factor that segregates a results metric from the others is one that guarantees they always be reviewed after the fact, having aggregated over a period of time—one week, one month, one quarter, or even one or more years. The time basis can vary for analysis purposes, but the results can't be changed because the performance window is closed. Let's take the example of sales in any industry where daily, weekly, or monthly sales may be too volatile or "lumpy" to be analyzed. By extending the measurement period, you can smooth over the lumps, or even identify seasonality—differences that might make them helpful in managing forward or more proactively. Results metrics are necessary to ascertain progress and can be useful in adjusting your tactical direction, and to steer your strategies. It's their longer, steadier point of view, and accuracy borne of hindsight that makes them easier to communicate effectively within the greater organization. To be clear, the greatest value of a result metric is in what it can teach you—just like a historical artifact.

Managing Metrics

Similar to results metrics, the factors that separate managing metrics include both evaluation time as well as the action or effect timing. With managing metrics, the review timing is usually shorter—weeks, days, hours, even minutes—with rapid commensurate action required in order to affect the end result. To explain more fully, we'll return to the sales example. In an industry where the final product might be perishable, daily or even hourly sales trends might be necessary for the management team to understand when to initiate promotions or change the amount of inventory they are creating or bringing in. Management metrics have a direct push-pull characteristic and they require tight alignment between the activity, the review timing, and the initiation of corrective actions for them to function usefully.

Predictive Metrics

It's important to keep in mind that rearward facing results are primarily useful for identifying and guiding strategic and corrective actions, and management metrics can be used to steer direction and mitigate problems. While all metrics are ultimately results, there are a precious few that can help predict the future by the way they are trending, or by how they contribute to those trends. You can expose their usefulness after investing some time to learn how their relationships work and what review timing is best. Because they have some predictive power, as opposed to providing after-the-fact results, the earlier you identify and respond to these metrics with management efforts, the more these "leading indicators" can guide you to improvement. Not all leading indicators are obvious, or even directly correlated; for example, a leading indicator to a safety metric may come from tracking the number of "near misses," coaching discussions, or even "at-risk" behaviors logged, whereas a leading indicator to sales may be the timing or pattern of responses (hits) to an internet marketing campaign. Predictive metrics are the most powerful of all for their ability to identify steering actions that can impact future results. The most commonly used predictive metric is sales forecasting. It often (but unfortunately not always) drives marketing actions, material purchases, human resource commitments, and other activities. Another option for sales might be internet inquiries. There are other examples; for employee wellness, your predictive options might be health care cost trends, safety incidents, or even trends for employee absenteeism. Predictive metrics require more discovery work to find, and the data often has to be "mined" for long periods of time before useful corollaries can be recognized. Nearly all global metrics should have some sub-level measures that have predictive power, and they are worth the effort to identify, measure, and act on.

Financial Metrics

Always a member of the key metric group, financial measurements have been left as a separate topic for our purposes here, primarily because not all organizations treat them as "public" measures. Although sharing critical financial information to the associate group may be preferred in some businesses, there are many valid reasons to limit distribution—such as insider stock sales for a public company. We've included only the basic financial measurements in our table **(see page 106)** to acknowledge their importance, but we'll exclude them from any at-length analysis or discussion. That said, the simplification methods we have reviewed to this point as well as some additional ones coming up, all apply to financial metrics as well.

Metric Response Cycles

Chapter seven introduced the concept of cycles of response as they apply to the structure and execution of your business processes. The concept also applies to your metric reviews because if the review timing is kept in sync with your priority checks, your ability to successfully steer the business with corrective or preventive adjustments will be timely enough to have an impact. I'll again pick on sales for the subsequent examples because nearly every business relies on it as a key metric. The term "metric response cycles" implies that the measurements and the response actions are inter-dependent. Since every metric data point has a limited useful life, the timing of data collection, review, and corrective action is critical and must take place within that time period. Most of the data occurs environmentally and is beyond your control—markets, people, conditions, and other things change constantly and can either affect the metric, its baseline, or even its definition. Equally, the ability of corrective actions to alter the causes of a performance problem also changes over time. Metric response cycles require you to identify the measurement and follow-up timing associated with each metric, and tightly coordinate the scheduling of your reviews to enable corrective or steering actions to have an effect.

Selecting Metrics

Finalizing your list of business metrics can require a bit of trial and error. A wide variety of measurements can be collected and reviewed depending on the specific type of business, so many that I won't even attempt a list. To get started, follow the high-level business themes to ensure that the interests of customers, stakeholders, and employees are supported. From there follow the common themes to determine what's important, and therefore what to measure. Of course, there are checks and balances to follow:

1. Maintain the top-level $SQDC^2+T$ themes! With the exception of Safety, it's critical that one metric doesn't receive preferential treatment over another, so identifying a key measurement along each theme adds balance to your measurement and review process, while keeping associates from all functions engaged in their attainment.

2. Align your metric baselines with the organization's key objectives and their initiatives. Each metric target should align with the achievement of a key objective, or you probably should consider not using it.

3. Triangulate to improve effectiveness (more about this below). Three points of reference help to legitimize the metric target.

4. Maintain the correct levels for communication, review, and initiation of actions tied to your metrics. In other words, keep them stratified by the level of the organization that can most effectively act on them. Top-level metrics will be reviewed and deployed publicly - organization-wide. First-level pareto metrics are reviewed at the senior staff level, within a function, or co-owned by more than one function; next-level metrics can be reviewed at a functional or department level; others might go all the way down to a work center or even an individual. It's important to understand that mixing the review and communication of multiple pareto levels just confuses the organization and causes associates to lose focus. The lower the level of the metric, the tighter should be the review and response group.

Triangulation

In ancient seafaring days, there were no GPS devices available to help determine your position on the open seas—in fact, if you go back far enough, even the simple compass didn't exist. In order to find their way across the vast expanses of ocean, navigators used a technique called triangulation. This involved the determination of direction and relative location by viewing the ships position as it was related to two other points—typically astronomical. Since astronomy had become a well-developed science in some cultures, the sun and stars provided ample information to set a general direction, providing of course you had some idea of where you were going in the first place. Today, GPS technology utilizes a similar technique called "trilateration" to describe their method of determining the user's position by correlating his position using the signals from the three closest GPS satellites. It's a much more accurate version of the same technique, and it's a concept that applies to your change initiative as well.

My use of triangulation has evolved with practice from many years running larger organizations. Today, it's a rare occasion where I can't go into a business and reduce what's being measured, allowing people to "dial-in" on the most critical performance indicators. In each case, their performance improves and the organization becomes more successful. Why do you suppose it works that way? Part of it lies in the ability to get the associates focused on what makes a difference in their performance rather than all of the ways they are being measured. Another important aspect that often goes unnoticed, is that the independent functions in a large business generally have the latitude to establish their own local metrics and include them in their functional objectives. These functional metrics can frequently fall out of alignment with the other organization-wide measures, and their timing doesn't always match with the key metrics in the business. The result is metric overlap, silo-based performance results, and misleading "cause-and-effect" relationships. Having too many metrics that aren't uniformly connected to the business objectives reduces focus and impairs performance.

Triangulation is used in two ways to manage metrics in business. The first is slightly different than the method used in ancient navigation. In this case, if two tracked metrics can provide a relative readout of another, then the need to measure the third isn't required unless there is a specific reason. It's a valid approach to separating the "must" metrics from a greater group of those which "can" be measured. Comparing all of the metrics in the selection set, as well as moving up and down through the pareto levels can help you to understand the way some metrics influence others and which ones are critical to measure. Let's look at a couple of manufacturing and distribution examples.

1. If on-time delivery for your business is good, but delivery from your suppliers is poor, then chances are good that you're holding too much purchased inventory. Does it mean you do or don't have to measure purchased inventory specifically? You don't absolutely have to, but it *is* a choice you can make as indicated by its performance and the relationship it has with your primary inventory metrics. You will always absolutely measure inventory, and purchased inventory is certainly a pareto level option, but attentive supply management will improve your purchased inventory and you can avoid breaking it out separately unless you find other reasons to do so.

2. Although labor efficiency and productivity are also common metrics, these too can be eliminated by monitoring labor input (manpower applied) and unit production output (takt attainment). For this, you have to understand the work content required to determine labor applied, but if labor input is correct, and unit output is to takt, productivity is nearly automatic. Labor efficiency on the other hand is a sub-component of productivity that is so easily manipulated it's nearly worthless as a metric. Aligning the correct inputs and achieving the expected outputs can effectively eliminate less useful measurements.

Triangulation also helps to eliminate cause-and-effect metric relationships. These occur when one metric directly or indirectly affects one or more other metrics. Measuring cause-and-effect metrics can be frustrating since actions taken on one affect the results of the others—a phenomenon that can confuse root-cause and corrective action efforts. Typically, these will occur when attempting to take measurement snapshots of indices that change during the process of taking that snapshot. Inventory is a common example of where this can be an issue because of the way it moves through its transactions.

The use of triangulation can enable a reduction in the overall metrics set and allow you to do a better job of closing in on those measures that actually drive the business performance. Whereas every business has key metrics that are essential to their daily function and are always measured, the pareto level metrics present opportunities where time can be saved and energy redirected.

Below is an example chart from manufacturing for measurement, communication, and review of metrics performance at multiple organizational levels and across each of the metric types. The key metrics are balanced among the categories that were identified as essential and reviewed monthly with the entire organization. Those metrics slated for daily review among the leadership team should receive daily action with resources deployed to mitigate performance deviations and keep the business on track. Finally, pareto level metrics are reviewed by the cross-functional working teams on a weekly basis. Although this is primarily for example purposes, it incorporates all of the concepts we've reviewed in this chapter.

Results - Metrics Review and Communications Plan			
	Key Metric (Monthly Review)	**Weekly Review**	**Daily Review**
Key Metrics: SQCD+G	**Results Scorecard**	**Pareto Level Metrics**	**Forecast / Diagnostic**
Safety / Wellness	Safety Incident Rates Absence Days (Wellness)	Injury type, Activity, Cost	Near Misses
		Days lost by inlury type	Preventive Actions Completed
Quality	Customer reported Quality Field Performance	Supplier Quality Warranty Returns	Internal Process Quality Internal Scrap
Delivery	Product / Service Delivery / Fulfillment to Customer Request	Forecast Accuracy	Internal - Daily Fulfillment
		Sales Trend by Product	Order Response Time
		Late Supplier Deliveries	Order Aging
Cost	Inventory Metric	Inventory by Value/Model	Daily Receipts
	Productivity or Value-add Metric	Staffing, Shipmts/Lbr Hr	Daily Cost Input / Relief
+ Key initiative	On-Time / On-Cost launch	Gate deliverables on time	As Identified
	Sales From New Product / Service	Sales by product to target	
Financial Performance Metrics	Total Sales	Team level financial reporting as defined by the business	Daily Sales (Shipments)
			Order Intake
	Profit		By Business Type
	Working Capital / Cash Flow		Inventory Receipts
Review Level:	Entire Organization (Public)	Process Mgmt Teams / Workcells	Management Team

Summary

"I just can't figure it out!" the apprentice carpenter said to the journeyman. "I've cut this board three times, and it's still too short."

Complex measurement systems breed mistakes, and though that may not have been the apprentice's problem, you need to ensure that your measurements and communications are clearly defined and synchronized. Once your key metrics are identified and you've triangulated your way to the critical sub-metrics, what else do you need to do? Find and focus on your predictive metrics as quickly as possible. Then track them in parallel with your results metrics to understand their relationships.

For most companies, the concept of predictive or leading indicators might seem to be a "Make You Happy" priority, but the reality is that they can have dilutive power over the problems which may also be "Eating" your lunch and eroding your results. The sooner you can focus on them, the faster you can accelerate improvement and begin to make magical progress.

As you review the lessons learned, take steps to ensure that no matter what is measured, you always make them meaningful by doing the following;

1. Choose your measurements carefully.

2. Construct the metric definitions so they are honest, simple and explainable.

3. Keep the key (public) metric list short: S (or W), Q, D, C, C^2+ T.

4. All metrics should have owners or champions assigned to them.

5. Always communicate and fully deploy the definition and purpose of the metric.

6. Consistently and visibly take timely action on all of the key metrics (for correction or improvement).

7. Stratify your pareto-level metrics, manage them at the most appropriate level, and review them one level up *only*!

8. Maintain an exception management process for sub-level metrics that are off-track.

9. Define your cycles of response so that your review and actions create a process improvement loop.

Chapter nine will look at yet another aspect of building sustainable systems: auditing to sustain and engage. Spreading out or deploying the responsibility for embedding new behaviors and an expectation for results is an essential element of making them habitual. Auditing can be a positive methodology for doing just that, and we'll look at the approaches to accomplishing this next.

I'll summarize my metrics philosophy with a couple of quotes of my own:

"Conducting measurement and review without taking related action is waste. Either cease measuring or act on the information."

And finally: "Pursuing the right metric target with the wrong timing will induce poor behaviors and unravel an improvement plan more quickly than is imaginable."

Chapter 9: "En-gage-ment!"

Involve Associates to Build Sustaining Behaviors

1. Involve

2. Engage

3. Standardize and Simplify

4. Audit

5. Reinforce

Expending immense effort containing and correcting our performance problems, defining and deploying our strategy, initiating a Lean implementation, installing a commonly understood metrics system, and communicating our progress with the team, yielded a number of improvements very quickly. Everyone in the organization was participating, and in spite of the crushing workload and related pressure, the momentum of our successes kept team morale quite high.

Now, we really needed to free up the leadership team and get them focused on long-range improvements. It was a task that had to be accomplished without diverting attention from what we had gained, destabilizing our fragile improvements. We would have to gradually cover the gaps in management presence with broader deployment to the rest of the organization, in order to sustain progress on our initiatives.

"Welcome everyone!" I announced to a group that included all members of the management team as well as hourly group leaders. "Let's take inventory of our accomplishments in terms of our business performance over the past six months." I flipped through six graphs showing marked improvement in each key metric; safety, delivery, quality, cost-management, and responsiveness. "This entire team has been instrumental in these improvements and you should congratulate yourselves with a round of applause." Everyone stood and clapped.

"Unfortunately, we are still in very fragile shape. The herculean efforts expended to drive rapid improvement will not be sustainable without some additional work as we try to cement our improvements in place. Today I'm again asking for your help in making them permanent. The challenge going forward is that even well-intended changes may have the ability to disrupt what we've just begun to do well, so we'll need to take steps to make sure we continue to benefit from what we've learned."

"As a staff, we have been discussing this part of the challenge from the first day, and as we developed our strategy, the process of doing so exposed a number of shortcomings in our deployment tactics. That said, each of the staff members has agreed to become mentors for a different aspect of our cultural change initiative. They will each explain their roles from here."

With that, Maria described the current work in process using "pull behaviors" and highlighted some of the successes we experienced. "Many of our processes related to customer response have been improved using this concept. Our responsiveness to disruptions in the order flow has been transformed and our delivery performance is significantly better. Now we would now like to take it a bit farther—across the entire organization. It isn't about making people act like drones, but rather raising their awareness level of abnormalities and equipping them to react accordingly."

Geoff followed her. "Our work with this process is still very limited, and we would like to deploy it more deeply into the organization. The next step required for effectiveness and stabilization is to engage everyone in the organization in the process at some level."

"Engagement and involvement are similar but different. Involvement means that we ask you to participate while engagement gives you more 'skin in the game' by letting you help build the process." Maria added.

Geoff returned to the microphone. "So, knowing what you know so far and based on your own exposure to Behavioral Pull, how can we create more "pull" to sustain our improvements from the greater organization.

"We're improving at documenting our processes, but I think that finishing the job would be helpful," Mark, one of the manufacturing engineers, said.

"Great comment!" Geoff replied. "But maintaining the accuracy of those documents can be a hassle. Does anyone have any ideas on how to do *that part* of it better?"

"We should have a change control procedure that is governed by the owner of the document," Mark responded.

"So, the answer is to identify the process-related document owners and their responsibilities?" Karen asked. "Good! How do we make sure that it happens? You know, people get busy and often don't get to the semi-repetitive daily tasks. Then it comes back to bite us later."

"Auditing works in the accounting world. Why don't we audit these new processes and documents?" asked Martha, the accounting manager.

"The auditing load can't fall on too narrow a group of people or it won't get done properly," offered another accounting team member.

"And a single group won't have the multiple perspectives necessary to do proper audits on different processes without training." Maria spoke up. "If we're really going to utilize 'pull behaviors' for auditing then at least some of that auditing will have to be done at a peer-to-peer level."

"So, we are really saying that we should engage more people in the auditing process in order to maximize its impact." Geoff replied.

"It will take much more than that! We'll need to standardize the audit process, simplify it as much as possible, make sure it's thoroughly deployed, and monitor and reinforce the findings." Jolene offered. "We do that in Accounting all the time, but it's always pretty complicated. If we want good results across the organization, we'll have to simplify the way we do it."

"I'd suggest some form of a layered auditing program. That will enable us to cover the entire process and deploy it organization-wide, engaging everyone." I said. "The system design part will have to be allocated between the function that owns the process to ensure we identify the correct audit steps, then we can come back together and work on the deployment plan."

After some discussion, the group agreed on a plan to introduce "layered" auditing as a strategy to solidify our progress. It would not only keep us consistent with our overall themes of maximized engagement and open contribution, but also expands the auditing coverage and strengthens our performance disciplines. Interestingly, the team suggested a couple of twists to a traditional auditing approach that would have significant value.

"I'm going to suggest that we stay away from auditing results, because they are already covered by our key metrics. Besides, reviewing results isn't proactive or timely enough to avoid problems. My thinking is that we should target the processes and related behaviors that feed-in to deliver those results." Jolene said, earning a favorable response from the team.

"And I'm going to recommend that we broaden the level of involvement and engagement to all associates, well beyond what might be done in a typical audit program." Geoff said. "Getting as many people engaged as possible will reduce an individual audit's scope and simplify it. It will increase the pressure on us to train people in their audit duties, and follow-up on the responses, but it will also help to create ownership through engagement and encourage peer-to-peer coaching by having associates audit each other's sustaining process steps. I think it will go a long way toward building sustaining behaviors through positive reinforcement."

Again, there was a positive response from the team, so we collectively decided that the individual staff members should assemble their functional audit teams and begin to delineate the audit steps.

Over the next couple of weeks, the groups spent a considerable amount of time identifying process results and behaviors that were considered to be more diagnostic in nature and when tracked or monitored, would be capable of alerting associates to the need for corrective action.

With the system designs completed and implementation nearing, we came back together to discuss our plans to roll out the program.

"I'm so proud of this team for all of the awesome work you have done. Have the functional discussions raised any concerns, or are we ready to go and implement?" Maria took the lead.

"I'm really worried about those situations where I or one of my team members might find something wrong with the way another teammate is doing their work, and that person gets mad at us for reporting it." One of the hourly team leaders said.

"We have thought of that." Geoff answered. "While I can't guarantee it will go perfectly, we're going to implement this level by level, taking great care to prove to people that no negative feedback will come out of it, only constructive solutions."

"We have training sessions scheduled for everyone in the facility including Positivity Coaching, Facilitation, and Conflict Avoidance, depending on your roles and responsibilities. The first few times feedback is given, it will be done in pairs, to make the coaching easier. This program is all about positive improvement." Maria said.

"We should also realize that if the audit standards are thoroughly rolled out and understood, then reinforced frequently through auditing and training updates, the problems should become less frequent, and people will be more accepting of the process." Maria closed the discussion on that note.

As was expected, the groups took to their tasks willingly enough and did a great job lining out the preparatory work and delivering the finished process to the greater organization. Consistent with our experience in the prior initiatives, the use of cross-functional associate teams to create our audit process earned tremendous credibility for the program. The teams designed the audit approaches, the training and screening programs, and the reward systems. They were then recruited to train the users, monitor the launch and fine tune their approach along the way.

The implementation started slowly, meeting a bit of resistance, mostly related to learning the skills of coaching associates through their struggles with peer-to-peer feedback. Everyone's individual objectives were altered to emphasize the need to manage and intervene and we took extra care to ensure that no one was penalized for a failure to adapt. Performance interventions were limited exclusively to instances where there was a failure to make an effort. Gradually we built momentum, and as the organizational behaviors began to match those we targeted, the performance gains also accelerated.

Thus far we've entertained numerous aspects of involvement and engagement, and yet there are still a few remaining. Both require incredible diligence to become culturally ingrained, and the problem usually begins at the leadership level, because it can only take one innocent "executive decision" to make a change in direction seem schizophrenic to the associate group. Absent a clearly communicated definition of the *why,* adjustments to your game plan can break down and disconnect any change efforts. Certainly, the leadership in any business has the authority to change direction, but their dependence upon the organization for support during transformation implementation stipulates a reasonable level of continuity. Involving associates in the decision process and engaging them in the implementation builds a commitment to deliver results and exponentially expands the brainpower they will add to problem solving, vastly increasing your odds of success.

Involve to Sustain

We'll start with involvement that, when applied to the problem-solving process, will both strengthen the organization's skills and increase the quality of the solution. Both are fundamental to sustainment, because implementing a solution that is designed by an involved team encourages them to take responsibility for the improvements, readily gaining acceptance and speeding deployment.

The best approach for keeping associates involved is to ensure that their role in the project, the behaviors you expect from them, and the leadership participation throughout the effort are *all* clearly defined. This is similar to the requirements we discussed under empowerment, where the definition of their role also clarifies their span of control, as well as the point when they should escalate a problem to the next level or function. Leadership support must always be accessible to take timely action in order for the system to sustain its effectiveness.

Consistent with the timing concepts covered in "cycles of response," your improvement initiatives must progress at a pace that is gently greater than the rate of organizational momentum, creating that needed "pull" on behaviors. To reinforce an earlier point: Moving too quickly leaves the organization disconnected, critical details unfinished, communications fragmented, and results lagging. I often refer to it as "leaving bodies behind!" Conversely, moving too slowly hampers the creation of organizational energy and momentum for your improvement efforts, causing you to underachieve. This is the point where no one really believes anything is changing. Monitoring and adjusting the pace of the effort to generate and maintain constant positive inertia is pivotal to sustaining your improvements.

Engage to Sustain

The fundamental difference between involvement and engagement is that, as a leader, you will consciously make the choice to involve others, while your associates will make the choice—both consciously and subconsciously—to engage. The effectiveness of your involvement efforts will determine your ability to "pull" associates in, and its success will depend on how well you create a compelling level of buy-in. Both the buy-in and the "pull" will materialize as an outcome of the way you empower, communicate, and stimulate the flow of change.

The motive to engage will take shape in the early stages of your improvement initiative, influenced by the methods you choose to deal with the early resistance that is always present. Anticipating the causes for a reluctance to participate, simplifying the technical message in order to neutralize complexity, and positioning all communications from the perspective of your associates, will allay their concerns and enlist engagement. You can close the deal by carefully defining the benefits of the effort in terms of what's in it for them, as well as what's in it for everyone. Keeping associates connected to the motives behind, and the benefits of your change initiative, while demonstrating management support across all activities, will best position you to advance the engagement efforts.

Standardize to Simplify and Sustain

Now, let's revisit the Lean tools, specifically *Standard Work* and *Jidoka*. As we reviewed in chapter seven, standard work insists that everything you do adds value for your customer and can be broken into three simple elements: major step (what to do), key points (what to watch out for) and reason why (why it's necessary, or the consequences of not doing it). All processes have both unique components and similarities, and standard work enables you to leverage those common elements through consistency of approach. Standardization has three byproducts that will substantially improve the organization's ability to sustain its improvements. First, the process commonalities make it easier for associates to learn across all of the processes, simplifying training and reducing the amount of time for them to come up to speed. This enables associates to move more fluidly between processes while remaining effective. Second, standardization reduces the amount of communication needed when changes are introduced to the processes, making it easier to keep them current. Finally, leveraging these commonalities can allow for a more rapid rate of improvement due to the synergies created across the business.

Jidoka, on the other hand, attempts to develop a habitual set of responses to business issues through the use of specially designed corrective action tools. These are Lean-based tools capable of counteracting or preventing performance abnormalities that can generate waste, deteriorate productivity, and threaten customer relationships through performance losses. Early stage Jidoka techniques are highly responsive, often providing containment measures rather than solutions, but they should evolve into preventive measures if given the correct attention.

Standardization is a difficult tool to stay abreast of, if for no other reason than it can run counter to our natural desire to create, refine, evolve, and improve the business. Improvement actions that generate isolated solutions can break down those standards and if merited, must be carefully integrated into the existing processes. Keeping improvements focused and connected across the organization so that standards evolve constructively and their benefits aren't diluted, takes tremendous discipline. The lesson ultimately proves that standardization is a simplifier, making your processes easier to live with and sustain so long as the drive for improvement doesn't allow complexity to creep back in.

Auditing for Sustainment

Perhaps attributable to its more traditional uses, auditing is one of the most underused and/ or misused practices in business. Surely there are financial and human resource professionals out there saying, "He must be out of his mind!" But if you've stuck with me this long, you already know there is a twist. For our purposes, let's simply define auditing as "third party verification of the performance of a process against its requirements." Although that definition makes it sound more like a glorified version of inspection, auditing differentiates itself by its more random frequency and a focus that goes beyond just the results of a process. When auditing is extended into the process functions, the results can be assured to more consistently meet the standard applied to them.

We will often relentlessly audit financial results and compliance history, always with a focus on how accurately the process rules were adhered to. The problem with these examples is that the timing of any results-based review combines with the nature of a compliance mandate to create a negative connotation (the "gotcha" effect) for those being audited. Further, the real-world impact is that the compliance activities associated with a scheduled audit are often crammed into the last few days prior to the scheduled audit event, elevating the stress and fear already present in the team due to the nature of the audit process, its feedback, and, in many cases, its consequences. For our uses, turning auditing from enforcement to reinforcement transforms it into a very positive motivator in the pull behavior tool kit, one that can change a culture and aid in sustaining improvement.

Positive Intervention – For a number of years, I've had the pleasure of working at an oil refinery in the Canadian Oil Sands Region. No organization takes safety as seriously as they do, and for good reason—failure can be catastrophic. These folks have, at one time or another, put together millions of work hours without a serious injury, and two of their cornerstone techniques involve behaviors and auditing.

Behaviorally, their method of moment-by-moment reinforcement utilizes the concept of intervention. When someone is observed working in an unsafe way, it is the observer's response-ability to step in and intervene to address the problem. In order to surround that effort with a positive theme, they expend a considerable amount of energy coaching everyone at every level of the organization as well as the contractors they hire that it's okay to intervene, establishing an expectation that even negative interventions can be delivered in as positive a fashion as possible. There is yet a further expectation on the part of the recipient that a respectfully delivered intervention is to be received respectfully. The entire site supports the practice with a zero-tolerance policy for any lack of courtesy from either side surrounding safety issues.

Although negative interventions must occur immediately as discovered, each member of the leadership team is required to counter every negative intervention with a specified number of positive ones. In a positive intervention, a worker is proactively thanked for being observed working safely, performing a safe act, or for assisting someone else to work safely, with some kind of reward, ranging from a sticker to a keychain or even a pocket knife or lighter. The intent of establishing the ratio is to drive a positive overall tone to the program, increasing its acceptance.

The intervention approach is supported with logbooks by an intense auditing methodology. All members of management are tasked with daily audit responsibilities for safe work practices as well as for compliance with personal protective equipment. They report their findings, maintain logbooks, and generate daily grade cards for the leading indicators of "risk-tolerant" behaviors, following them up the next day with site-wide awareness and auditing themes designed to address the largest problems, getting the attention of everyone involved. The auditing data is used to feed a series of predictive metrics, which are aggressively acted upon.

Establishing a quota for positive interventions is the magic bullet that moves their safety approach from a reactionary one with a negative tone, to a proactive one with a positive tone. It's a requirement for their associates to issue a favorable ratio (two to four) of positive interventions for each negative one they issue. That has helped them avoid many injuries and has a side benefit of building engagement by "pulling" the behaviors of everyone involved.

Reinforce

Using Pull Behaviors: In chapter six, the "Pull Behaviors" process was seeking to identify and solicit those behaviors that will directly support (and therefore sustain) an improvement. These are especially useful to close gaps in three areas: process execution, abnormality response, and team-based problem solving. A thorough job of standard work should strengthen process execution by virtue of the nature of its content, and Jidoka techniques will set in place fundamental practices for providing timely and competent response to abnormalities. Sustaining team-based approaches for initiatives stretching from launch through implementation helps to establish a forum for peer-to-peer coaching and layered performance reviews, both triggered by auditing activities and metric checks.

Establishing audit points for key performance indicators at the beginning of your change initiative can help expose and close gaps in process execution. Examples of this include audit points for incoming service calls, materials receipts, receivables, customers in line, and elapsed time through a process step. Periodic monitoring of process inputs provides a clearer indication of the need for preventive or corrective action, whereas auditing abnormality responses can help to confirm that process problems are correctly resolved within the necessary response-cycle. Some examples might include dropped sales calls, generation of nonconforming product, machine stoppages, late order fulfillment, and tardy payables.

Team-based problem-solving opportunities can be identified during project reviews. They might be sourced from customer-submitted issues, or may arise from issues discovered during the course of process execution and abnormality response. The time to completion and quality of problem resolutions will also offer up auditing options that can yield peer-to-peer coaching opportunities and include performance feedback.

Auditing alone doesn't create pull behaviors, but it will strengthen and accelerate them substantially when performed with the proper timing and constructive intent. Turning the audit function from a practice that exposes a failure to one that reinforces task performance within the rules is a more proactive approach that emphasizes positive feedback and timely coaching, making it both constructive and instructive. Process failure is replaced with preventive actions, while individual failure is avoided through communication, training, and visual cues. Emphasis on that last element of standard work, *the reason why*, becomes the glue that encourages associates to stick to the process rules and helps to sustain them. The list of "things done poorly" metamorphoses itself into an inventory of finely tuned improvements, and it's all an outcome of simply taking a different angle on how you view and present it. The further in the process you extend your auditing, the more successful the preventive efforts will be in lowering the number and severity of the problems you experience.

Expanding the audit base: Broadening associate involvement in an auditing process has two benefits. First, more auditing can be performed across a wider spectrum of activities, adding capacity for proactive process reviews. Second, with more participants, each audit can become smaller in scope, making them easier to perform effectively. A common deployment option is "layered auditing", a technique that refers to audits that are performed by different levels of the organization (from group leaders to senior managers). The positive aspect of this approach is the engagement of all levels of the organization in obtaining a multi-functional perspective of performance. Its greatest limitation is that the breadth of auditing will be restricted by the amount of resources that are committed to the program, and the upper levels of the organization often participate too infrequently to have the desired impact. Layered auditing only reaches maximum effectiveness if every organizational level participates to the extent necessary to achieve the program objectives.

The first requirement of broadened audit involvement is for each employee to perform some type of audit function. It should be limited to something within their capabilities—an example might be as simple as area 5's (workplace organization) compliance to plan—but all associates must play a part. It's this participation that helps create the momentum for cultural change, bringing with it frequent reinforcement for understanding the organizations goals.

The expanded capacity provided to the audit program allows you to broaden beyond compliance and into both preventive and sustaining activities, accelerating the impact of the improvement programs.

Team based auditing can enable a simpler scope for each auditor, expanding to all critical aspects of process performance. While a number of approaches for audit team structure are possible, centering them either on natural functions or even the specific strategic initiatives both serve as excellent points of focus.

By taking the extra care to proactively audit your processes and deliver the findings constructively while providing support systems for the peer-to-peer positive interventions and coaching, the road to success will be far easier to travel.

Lean Assessment: A sizeable part of my career has been spent developing and launching Lean Assessment programs. One of the companies I worked for established a tool for measuring and enforcing compliance to the corporate Lean implementation schedule as its primary objective. It took that turn because of the reticence a few of its key executives had shown in embracing the corporate Lean initiative as fully as they should. The assessment process was initiated at the CEO level to accelerate the adoption of Lean practices across the corporation. A requirement to increase an organization's minimum "Lean Assessment" scores was imposed first in the manufacturing facilities and then in the administrative offices. It worked well enough to improve the behavior of some of the executives in question, but failed to help Lean take root on a grander scale. Although the assessment process did a great job of evaluating Lean tools usage, it struggled to have an impact on the cultural behaviors that needed to change, leaving a lot of opportunities for transformational improvement on the table.

Similar to some audits, the findings from an assessment merely reflected a snapshot of the process's current state of effectiveness. As I looked through the second draft of my fifth iteration of Lean Assessment (reviewing the point scores and criteria to see if they were properly aligned), I was still looking for a way to make the assessment feedback more useful. It was then I realized that an assessment shouldn't simply provide a score, but rather a set of specific recommendations for the subject's improvement based on its observations. If the assessment identifies key areas needing improvement, then the evaluation criteria itself can serve as a path to improvement, or, better yet, a program roadmap. With that, the audit results were turned into a step-by-step guidebook to explain how to accelerate the Lean transformation. That change in its "angle of approach" moved my Lean Excellence Assessment Process (LEAP) beyond a mere benchmarking tool to become a template for evaluation and action planning.

Summary

The power and value of auditing grows significantly when it's spun toward proactive content and positive intervention. It becomes a support mechanism for behavioral engagement with some very effective improvement tools as its outputs: feedback, involvement, and forward planning. Like the Lean tools, auditing must be embraced by the organization and deployed broadly through "layering." This ensures that managers are always in a contributing auditor role rather than just a leadership one, facilitating improvements to their processes instead of directing outcomes. If the output of an audit is used to develop a road map to reach the next level, it will be more constructively received than if simply presented in the form of a list of deficiencies.

Finally, the value of engagement should never be discounted. Not only does broad audit engagement help accelerate the positive contributions, but it can also develop technical and leadership skills while deploying a more uniform set of expectations for all.

Sustaining your gains is essential to the successful evolution of any improvement initiative, but it's the most difficult aspect of every one of them. Unless they are properly dispatched, old behaviors will rapidly creep back in to replace the new ones. Facilitating sustainment is a function of maintaining a pace of positive momentum, using creative methods to involve and engage, emphasizing standardization, and building audit systems that engage broadly in support of the changes by encouraging the desired behaviors.

You can further enhance the effectiveness of audit processes by acknowledging positive contributions. Rewards, recognition, and celebrations are powerful reinforcements that provide sufficient motivation to build team-based action and accelerate progress.

Chapter 10: Consistentize

Business Systems that Secure Long-Term Performance

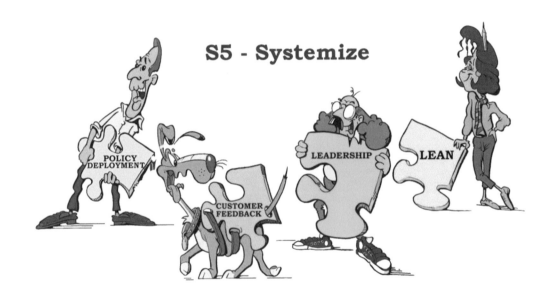

S5 - Systemize

1. Defining Core Processes

2. Confirming Process Performance

3. Assign Process Ownership

4. Aligning Metrics

"Welcome, folks!" Geoff was batting leadoff for the staff as he addressed the team. "I have the pleasure of getting our first business transformation celebration underway and am going to ask my teammates on our staff to set the tone by reminding you of what we accomplished during this past year."

Dick rose and spoke, "Not only have we saved our account standing with several major customers, but we've actually grown our business with them by nearly 15 percent. At the same time, we've redesigned four major product platforms and successfully launched two of those to enthusiastic customer acceptance." Murmurs of approval were heard around the room. "And, as a side bonus, we've reduced our engineering order-processing time from seven days to just two."

Geoff stepped back up. "Our safety incidents have dropped more than 75 percent and our goal of zero is in sight. We have also driven delivery performance up to over 91 percent and climbing."

"And we've done all of that with one-third less inventory," Janet added.

Maria moved to a podium. "Fifteen percent of our associates have completed a personal development course, and eight percent have improved their performance levels, based on their end-of-year assessments. What an awesome job all of you are doing!"

Karen added, "Our profitability has improved nearly four percentage points in what many agree was a down market!"

I returned to the podium. "I'm very proud of all of you for your accomplishments, but the truth is, we've only begun our overall transformation. I commend each of you for your focus, determination, and loyalty. Everyone in this room, and across the entire company, has made a positive contribution to this amazing turnaround. Well done!"

I led the group in giving itself a round of applause.

"Naturally, we can't relax or rest on our laurels and assume the job is done. Because in fact, although improvement is a never-ending challenge, it *is* self-rewarding. Knowing this, my new goal is to guide you to improve on what you've already begun to do well. This morning, I'd like to review our primary process initiatives for the coming year. By doing this as a group, hopefully everyone will understand how critical these are for our future success."

I shifted gears for a moment and hefted a sheath of handout pages that would be distributed to them.

"One of the byproducts of the hard work we've undertaken in turning this business around is that we have isolated a number of core business processes that have been elevated to a management level. In other words, we'll ensure the key metrics and certain sub-level metrics for those processes are reviewed and acted upon on a daily, weekly, and monthly basis. This plan has the nickname of "Consistentize" and its intent is for us to become consistently improving performers through disciplined follow-up and response to performance variations in these core processes that drive our business.

"To develop plans and objectives for the next few years, the staff and I assembled a larger group of the management team to collect our own ideas, ask customers for their input, and to look within the corporation or outside to our markets for benchmark opportunities. What we came up with was this list of core processes that we'll use to accelerate our transformation across the business. I'll lead a process called Leadership. The goal of this leadership process is to improve the way we establish our long- and short-range business plans, making sure all of the appropriate input is considered and that our objectives are sufficient to make us a top tier performer in our markets. We'll call the process PDMR. Simplistically, we're going to do a much more thorough job of planning, deploying (or Involving), measuring, and reviewing the performance of our financial planning, strategy execution, and supplier management sub-processes by using specific review and improvements cycles for each.

"Now I'd like the individual members of the staff or another member of management who have agreed to serve as process champions for each of the remaining processes to step up front and present an overview of their processes next."

I motioned for Jolene to come forward and describe her role in the process improvement effort.

"I'll be the champion for our strategy deployment process. It's an important process for developing and rolling out both our strategic and annual tactical objectives, as well as measuring our progress to those goals. We will outline the projects we will use to achieve our objectives and assign implementation teams to each one."

Dick stepped up next. "My process is Customer Focus, and it will track how we listen to our customers and use their input to improve. We haven't done the best job of listening to them and acting on what they have been telling us, so one of the sub-processes is designed to fast track customer input so we can decide how to act."

Maria was right behind him, "My Associate Excellence team will work with a new process called ADAPT, standing for Associate Development, Assessment, Performance, and Talent management process. In it we'll work on how we evaluate our individual and team performance, then determine how to use the feedback to determine training needs and drive personal development."

"I'll be directing our product development process implementation of APQP, Advanced Product Quality Planning," John said. "We've already done a lot of brainstorming around this, and it's definitely going to be an exciting year."

"Performance of our manufacturing and service processes will be my area," Geoff added. "We are tasked with implementing Lean Enterprise to improve our own process performance and integrate the input of our customers and stakeholders."

"Finally, my team will take us to world class levels of market and customer response," Janet promised. "If there's one thing we've learned this past year, it's that if the customers aren't satisfied, nothing else really matters. So, my team and I intend to become even more fanatical in our efforts to serve customers by using Sales and Operations Planning (S&OP) to improve order response time, reduce costs, and deliver higher quality."

I nodded approvingly. "You have all done an excellent job. Each of these initiatives will remain focused on a single process and a few sub-processes. Each of the process champions will assemble a cross functional team that will give us a 360-degree view of our process performance. They will monitor the performance metrics and implement changes that will maintain our progress on our overall improvement initiatives."

A hand went up. "How are we going to do all of this around our normal work?" one of the young engineers asked.

"Fair question," I said. "We believe that by developing new processes that are leaner than the old ones, we'll take a lot of non-value-added work out of the current ones freeing up some of peoples time. Eventually, workloads may actually be reduced, but in the interim, we are all going to have to try a little bit harder to balance day-to-day responsibilities with our highest project priorities. If necessary, we'll reschedule when have to. Are there any other questions?"

Nobody offered a response. "Very well. Since no one ever wants to stand between you folks and a party, let's get it going." With that, I excused them and we moved on to celebrate a transformational year.

Under normal circumstances, an organization's natural ability to initiate and absorb change won't be rapid enough for it to adapt and avoid collateral damage when its own markets experience upheaval. That's when a change initiative can help reduce your vulnerabilities. As explained in the concept of cycles of response, the failure to accelerate your rate of change to match the transformation taking place in your markets can be catastrophic. One lesson painfully learned during the financial crisis of 2008 is that size won't help. Some very large corporations folded their tents due to over-exposures that were exploited by the unprecedented market conditions of that crisis.

Most businesses are complex. The combination of products, processes, markets, customers, supply chains, computer networks, organizational structures, development plans, facilities, and even their role in their communities can all contribute to turn something that might have begun simply into an entity that is extremely process diverse. Well-intended people in one area of the business might implement corrective actions that negatively impact other areas of the business. The impacted groups then apply another layer of corrective actions (or band aids) to fix their new problem, which in return might alter the effectiveness of a different segment of the organization. The pursuit of cause-and-effect continues to move in circles until systemic problems develop. Because stop-gap fixes are unable to remedy the progressive disruption, a more severe realignment is required.

I saved Consistentize until nearly the end, not because you won't introduce stabilizing behaviors throughout the course of your process improvement initiatives, but as you begin to produce results, you'll want to make them "stick" and keep them coming. Identifying your key processes and modifying them to support the changes imposed by your initiatives is the perfect way to ensure sustainability. In this chapter, we'll apply all of the previously discussed sustainment methods to the way you structure and execute your critical business processes.

As may have been implied, we've been assembling the real sustainment methodology step-by-step as we progressed through the book. The best results spawn from well-constructed and tightly-managed processes, and it's the integrity contained within their design that allows sustainment to build. We've talked about how to develop sustaining behaviors that are supported with visual process triggers, requesting action in ways that trained associates can understand and respond to. The consistency of the response is supported by the training and reinforced by multi-level process "key points" and metrics that are audited by the entire organization. This holistic approach is completed by an expectation for results that is deployed organization-wide, all the way to the individual level, to build performance discipline—that's what it takes to sustain.

Driving change while expecting consistent results might seem like an oxymoron; the two forces seem to be in opposition. The reality is that you will typically invoke a change initiative because you want to create consistently improving results, and although there might be an occasion where you will accept a short-term performance loss to gain a potentially significant improvement, it usually isn't necessary. If you're driving change with an expectation of stabilizing results, then you're most likely driving the wrong kind of change.

The greatest risks introduced with any type of change initiative come from their ability to disrupt embedded, comfortable behaviors—people's habits: how they think, act, and respond on a daily basis. Obtaining consistently improving results is a matter of finding out what must be changed to drive improvement and then focusing on *only* those things, while at the same time protecting and leveraging any good embedded process-driven behaviors. Alfred North Whitehead once said, "The art of progress is to preserve order amid change and to preserve change amid order." His statement supports the idea that a leader must take pause to find the good in any organization and leverage it, focusing the change effort on only that which needs improvement; anything more is unnecessarily disruptive and will certainly cause *waste!*

Early in my career, I believed strongly in "change for the sake of change." My reasoning was that it could be useful as a force to break people out of their daily habits or comfort zones. I often used the example of placing an obstacle in the employees' entrance that would force them to choose a different path to their work stations, getting them to think consciously about something they otherwise would have done reflexively. Throughout the years my temperament has altered, helping me to realize that change that isn't supported by tangible needs can damage the credibility of the change effort. The best approach is to introduce change where it will do the most good without wasting resources or unnecessarily creating angst (resistance). If you fail to do so, the behaviors you want to disrupt will become the ones that rise up to create resistance to the changes.

No matter how strong your sustainment methods are, they will be ruined by inconsistent management or systems that don't perform to expectations. Getting consistent improvement from a change effort starts with a set of critical core processes that will serve as your management "constant." Let's define them, for now, as the processes that exist commonly in nearly every business: taking customer orders, fulfilling customer needs, managing cash, and developing employees. These processes control the pace of day-to-day performance by the way they "Consistentize".

Define Your Core Processes

How are core processes identified? Often times they become defined intuitively based upon the business type. Some processes are driven by industry standards, and some are even mandated through regulatory compliance. For the "basic" core processes that almost everyone should have, I favor a list that is derived from the Malcolm Baldrige Performance Excellence Award that promotes a more standardized methodology focused around the needs of the business and its stakeholders.

The Baldrige process seeks to evaluate the performance of a business from the way that it manages processes within the following seven categories: Leadership, Strategy, Customers, Measurement Analysis and Knowledge Management, Workforce, Operations, and Results. It specifically asks how the applicant goes about developing and using their processes that fall under each category, and it would seem logical that at least one key process for each should exist. That's actually a great place to start, except that it's possible to have more than one critical process under each of the seven categories, and every process doesn't have to be key to the business. Key processes should be designated as such because the way you manage them can have a make-or-break impact to a business.

The first process on the list is Leadership. Building a process around daily Leadership activities might seem a bit odd, and in truth, many businesses I've been a part of do not formally have a process called leadership. But making a process out of it is the most appropriate way to build consistency into your own management efforts, and that leadership presence will greatly help to set organizational performance on an upward trend. When a leadership team methodically manages the way it sets priorities and the expectations regarding them, it conveys a message of discipline, integrity, and dependability to the entire organization. My own example process that I've used in seeking sustainable leadership results is PDMR: Plan, Deploy, Measure, and Review. The planning step should take place at three levels: strategic, annual operating, and organizational development. Linking the deliverables among all three will help to connect your strategies to your tactics while shaping the organization to deliver them both. The results phase contains an improvement and feedback loop for the entire process and enables synergetic adjustments, as PDMR is deployed through the use of strategic planning sessions and operating progress reviews, as well as in the organization's development processes.

To accomplish this, a process similar to the one used in our proprietary Business 5s Process (B5s) will move you beyond planning into execution. In an indirect fashion, much of the simplicity of B5s has already been described within the context of this book. The first "S," Strategy, also comprises the second critical business process and derives its approach from the widely accepted "Strategy Deployment" process, which engages the organization in developing or refining its market and business strategy. The strategy is then divided into initiatives and assigned metrics, before being deployed cross-functionally. Generally, it takes two processes to fully cover your strategic needs: one for strategy development that covers multiple years and the other, a tactical initiatives deployment process (TID), that deploys and monitors your strategy related operating objectives for the current year.

The Customer process seeks to ensure that you have sufficient focus to ensure all customer needs are fulfilled, not with an ordinary sales process, but with one that will take a broader view of the satisfaction of customer needs. For our purposes, the requirements/ideas/feedback (RIF) process asks how the design of products and/or services actually considers and then fulfills customer needs. The process structure initiates with an exercise to identify customer needs, research the appropriate market benchmarks, and establish internal specifications. Next comes an ideation phase where customer and other stakeholder needs are cataloged and solutions are developed to be fed back into the strategic and operating plans. Finally, all sources of customer feedback should be constantly recycled to ensure that your metrics for their satisfaction remain relevant. It's also best if you triangulate between the internally defined list of market needs, the list of customer-defined requirements, and your set of "other" objectives generated for the business.

Once you have formulated your change initiatives, they should pass through three filters. The first and most heavily weighted filter is customer requirements: anything that doesn't address customer requirements should be considered expendable. There are reasons for working on something that doesn't satisfy customer needs in the short term, such as developing a product ahead of the market, but clear justification is required if they are to receive priority for resources before you commit those resources. The specific needs of the business and its internal stakeholders is the second filter. Customer programs must be appropriate for the needs of the business, and where they can't be, special scrutiny must be applied. The final filter is market and regulatory requirements. It's important to ensure that competitiveness is defined by the market rather than a single customer, even when your business is biased toward a limited customer base. Any regulatory considerations must be clearly understood and resolved.

Business Systems

In the context of the Baldrige criteria, the processes associated with the seven categories comprise a complete business system. After establishing processes for leadership, strategy, and customer needs, process number four transitioned from one of mid-level importance to a mission-critical level, just in the past couple of years. The management and security of business data has come under constant attack, and in today's world, demands much more attention and effort than in the past. It's also a clear reminder that business strategies must continually adapt to the assault of changes coming from their environments. The sub-categories might include order management, planning and inventory controls, time management, organizational communications, and accounting systems. The complete list is indigenous to the specifics of any particular business, but they should combine as a whole to enable you to manage market response and support your Response-Ability to all stakeholders.

Keeping a Workforce performing at its best goes far beyond simply assembling a set of metrics with a review process to manage them. Improving the skills of your associate resources necessitates a comprehensive organizational development process that cross-checks against business needs and addresses multiple aspects of performance. The Business 5s process for associate development is called ADAPT: Associate Development, Assessment, Performance, and Talent management. ADAPT ties objective and metrics performance to leadership, technical, and interpersonal competencies with disciplined performance review cycles to generate developmental actions. The one certainty is that with the current dearth of people with available skills on the market, your investments in associate development should also be complemented with equal attention to employee retention programs.

Of all the business process categories, operations covers the most ground and offers the most variable scope depending on the type of business. Some process examples might include: product/service development, launch management, new accounts management, perishable goods reordering, retail inventory verification, Lean Enterprise engagement, Production Operations, and Sales and Operations Planning. Also called S&OP, I was once convinced it stood for: Surprise! and Operations Panics! The list of possibilities is only limited by the diversity of the businesses utilizing the approach. Your final process list should focus on the specific nature of your business, then align with the timing and actions of the rest of your processes.

Managing a market response model is something very few organizations seem to think about, but it can make a vast difference in the success of any business. Initially, it requires blending customer requirements with market benchmarks to find the competitive response target for a given market.

Once you have defined your customer response needs, cycles of response can be employed across all aspects of the business to make sure that the individual processing and operating cycles are capable of matching those needs. From that point, emplacing a management process that utilizes timed review cycles that align with market needs helps to sustain a competitive edge.

Finally, having dedicated so much of this book to the topic of metrics, the last category of Results refers to the methods used to monitor and prioritize activities in order to leverage the improvement trends generated by the other business processes. For my purposes, managing results is simply an outgrowth of the way you review and deploy metrics. First, remember to use simplified and clearly defined versions of the headline $SQDC^2+T$ metrics at the organizational level: S (safety) *or* W (wellness), Q (quality), D (delivery), C^2 (internal/external cost), + T (time). Second, make certain your reviews are routinely scheduled and that all metrics and sub-level metrics are assigned to an owner or champion. Finally, every metric review should specifically include an improvement loop that utilizes process feedback to confirm problem resolution, as well as refine and improve the process that feeds that metric.

As you set the tone for process improvement, limit your specific instruction *only* to a mandate for simplicity of approach and solutions. You'll have to constantly stay on top of your teams to keep them focused on process alignment and objective metrics, so that the operating disciplines can build sustainment.

Confirm Process Performance

Achieving consistent results begins with thorough approach and deployment. To establish your approach, you should first review the results history and verify that it reflects what's required for both the business and for your improvement initiative. Carefully examine the results' definition as well as the quality of the reported data. If adjustment to either one is needed, they should be made and incorporated into your process. Take great care to retain and leverage all best practices as well as great performances—they will help to energize engagement through the momentum of success. Lastly, confirm the existence of both measurable feedback and actionable criteria to use in closing the improvement loop.

With the approach to achieving results clarified, it's time to do a deployment check. Broad deployment and participation in metrics improvement are essential to ensure organizational alignment and objective achievement. All segments of the organization should be equally engaged in attainment of the objectives, because just as a watch won't work if all of the gears don't mesh precisely, neither will your team.

Extend the positive momentum by publicizing your significant team and individual contributions in a way that galvanizes the effort. Any progress-reporting behaviors that might be confusing should cease. As well, all deviations from process, reporting, and performance standards should be limited by defining them in terms of "when to" and "when not to." Finally, when rewarding behaviors, make sure you separate innovation from achievement and attainment. Though all are valuable, they truly have unique effects on the organization, draw on resources separately, and generate rewards on different timelines.

Define Process Ownership

Previously we covered the need to assign owners or champions to each of the seven (or more) key business processes. This referred to the need for both functional process owners as well as leadership champions. Many processes will already have a natural, functional owner: payables falls under accounting, sales aligns to sales and marketing, production attainment belongs to the Operations group, and so on. Some processes may share ownership across functions, with ownership defaulting to whichever function can trump the other(s) with regulatory or other specific responsibilities. Functional process owners are assigned responsibility to refine and monitor process performance through the assistance of a key process team, and to adjust its processes definition and structure to maximize its effectiveness.

The leadership champions play a somewhat different role. They are needed to conduct high level performance reviews and process audits that confirm functionality and effectiveness. They may also serve as facilitators when process issues require external involvement from senior leadership or consultants, and sometimes even customers. The leadership champion reviews and approves process improvements while providing the team with business level feedback.

The cross functional team for each key process champion is made up of the process leaders or owners for each of the applicable sub-processes, or the appropriate customers of the process metric. This group should use business process improvement (BPI – similar to Lean Kaizen) techniques to initially map and document the process flow and the relationships of the sub-processes, confirming that they satisfy all prescriptive requirements, such as regulatory, corporate, or customer compliance. The sub-process leaders should also conduct bi-annual or annual reviews of process effectiveness covering performance data, customers and key user input, audit results, and the use of other feedback to drive improvements.

There are two vital benefits of the key process management approach. First, cross-functional team involvement retains organizational focus around the transformational objectives through their engagement and broader deployment. Second, the assignment of process ownership and the reviews incumbent to it, serve to close the improvement loop for each business process. It's this review-and-improve loop that allows the processes to evolve and remain effective.

Align Actions and Metrics

The need for a business-level result is usually what defines a key process and many of its elements. Throughout this book we've stressed the need to establish and maintain alignment between activities, results, and time because of their inter-dependencies. That said, it should come as no surprise that each key process and sub-process will require at least one metric to ensure that its effectiveness is represented by a result. Process-specific metrics help steer the actions of the improvement teams, and ensure their effectiveness and success. While most of these metrics will evolve from the processes themselves, others may require triangulation as well as additional intervention to create a useful measurement. The teams and their leadership champions will perform this task most effectively.

Summary

I've covered a lot of ground under the theme of "consistentize." In the addendum, you will find the basic flow charts for each of the key processes discussed in this chapter. Certainly, these can be expanded as needed by your individual business. No matter what approach you use, identifying the key processes that drive your business is an important step to solidify the improvements as they begin to materialize. Follow it up by integrating the needs of your change initiative into their process structures, engage your associates in managing them, and install metrics to monitor their progress; and you will close the loop on consistent improvement.

I'm sure some of these concepts may sound more complex than they really are, but it's really their simplest forms that are most powerful in application. The power comes from disciplined execution of the basics. Advocate a focus on core processes, measure only what you need to, engage everyone to understand how the metrics drive business performance, and use it all as a body of knowledge to manage the individual pieces at the best level to sustain the simplicity. Once these skills are mastered, your team will be more readily engaged and able to keep up. That's what makes it possible to preserve the order amid change and drive change amid order.

Chapter 11: Connecting the Dots

Adding it all up for Extreme Business Excellence

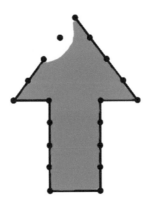

"You can't connect the dots looking forward: You can only connect them looking backward. So, you have to trust that the dots will somehow connect in the future."

Steve Jobs

I've used the phrase "connect the dots" in my management reviews for many years, so when I found this quote by Steve Jobs, it seemed like the right one to open this chapter with and to emphasize a point! That point is that if you want the dots to connect in the future, you will need to stay engaged and steer the pattern as it develops. Otherwise they won't connect into a clear picture.

After reading through this book, it seemed to me that my ability to maintain simplicity was elusive, so I decided to add this chapter as a review and summary of all of the individual concepts to "Connect the Dots!"

Lead with Vison!

Leadership is a trait that I've always felt was more bred than learned, and it isn't always well done. We all have our own idea of what a good leader is—probably formulated largely from our own experiences. One thing is for certain: If you are going to take a substantial organization through a significant change event successfully, the organization will have to believe in you. Fail to win them and you may achieve some level of success, but you won't achieve an optimized business objective.

It is impossible to over stress the need for you to play a visible role in the formulation of your vision for the company and engage others along the way. Seek input, introduce your own ideas, blend them all into the right message, and convey it to the organization in a way that energizes them. Even in the direst circumstances, once you are able to contain the bleeding, you'll need to formulate a winning strategy. Take the recent proclamations of a "retail-apocalypse." Many of the large retail chains have continually turned over their top managements in the face of Amazon's reinvention of the market. Why are so many of these management teams unsuccessful? Because not one of them has taken a bases-loaded whack at reinventing themselves. Sure, they will tell you that they are with store facelifts (oops, Amazon doesn't have a store—at least until recently), new promotions, free shipping (already done), and many other ideas, but the bottom line is that they are still a giant leap behind and losing ground quickly because of a lack of momentum. Even historic brands can't avoid the damage; Sears sold off both the Craftsman[R] and Die Hard[R] brands just to stay almost solvent, but may not be enough to turn their fortunes around.

Whatever vision you develop, make sure it can rise to the challenge, because only then will it engage your associates, and that is your best chance to win.

Assess and Engage!

Begin the engagement process with a careful situation assessment, involving your team in both the assessment activity and the establishment of early improvement objectives. Whether you're a newcomer to the business or a seasoned veteran, the collective understanding of its needs within the existing organization are superior to your own "one-eyed" perspective, and they should be allowed to play a role in the identification of potential solutions. Their participation is a key to facilitating "buy-in" and ensuring effective solutions and implementation.

I created the term Response-Ability years ago to emphasize the importance of being responsive to the greater needs of the business. A senior leader will have both the duty and the capability to align the entire organization in pursuit the needs of the business. The initial step in that effort is to get the leadership team to admit to the real condition of the business—a "confession of reality." It's the only way to get them working on the most urgent problems and also serves as an initial motivator—their contribution to a successful outcome.

Broadening involvement to everyone in the business expands the work "enterprise-wide" and enables thorough process solutions that can better address the business issues while attending to your customers or markets with optimal effectiveness. First, try to understand and address the many things that distract from their commitment—those influences that source from outside and inside the organization. Your path to success builds from consistency of leadership in setting expectations, identifying approaches, and maintaining engagement; in other words, organizational focus. Engaging the entire organization in the development of a vision keeps it from being "yours" and is a critical aspect of its credibility. It takes more than that to get the vision "rooted" to reality however.

Prepare!

"Rooting" the vision to reality makes it appear real, more attainable, and far less the "hallucination" that it might seem otherwise. That appearance of reality comes in part not only from the preparatory information used to frame it, but from a carefully planned approach to its achievement that combines a realistic pace of activities that will achieve the improvement milestones that encompass all of the business needs.

The more broadly you deploy your change initiative, the more likely its chances of success. Broad assignments of the initiative-related activities engage associate participation and builds interest by virtue of their involvement. Keep them abreast of changes driven by external forces and your adjustments to them. Continually updating results helps to maintain their interest during any "course corrections" your change initiative might require.

At its outset, you'll have to estimate and understand the impact of the changes on your organization. How significantly are you altering the core business? Is it enough? Will customers be affected? In the right way? How many people are involved internally and in what ways?

Answering these questions will give you an idea of the "mass" you're attempting to move, and how much force (resources + engagement) will need to be applied.

Successful change initiatives aren't just launched—they are the product of thorough preparation. Sizing up the potential impact of yours can be accomplished using directional estimates for the project workloads as well as the resources necessary to support the "bill paying" activities that must remain ongoing. In the same way that a good football coach will relentlessly prepare for a game, you'll need to prepare for your change initiative. Just as the coach will do a thorough inventory of player skills, one that includes existing capabilities as well as other potential options they may offer individually, he must also try to understand where his personnel might not adequately match up with those of the competition, and make appropriate adjustments or formulate contingency plans. Your own team assessment should thoroughly cover skills present and performance history, as well as identify any skill or performance gaps that can be addressed through associate development or personnel changes.

Before rolling out your initiatives, you should inform the organization of the vision and its overall objectives. Their participation and commitment will build from a trust that derives its strength from broad involvement, accurate measurement, and clear, timely communication of progress. Celebrate their achievements against the goals, while also allowing for timely game plan adjustments to change priorities and mobilize resources.

Prioritize!

Establishing priorities during a change initiative is one of the most critical aspects to its success, and they are highly dependent upon the condition of the business at launch. A business that's performing poorly and at risk of losing key customers must focus very hard on the "Things that will Kill them" to avert catastrophe. At the same time, they must avoid getting caught up in focusing purely on survival or else the basic business tasks will fail and the change initiative will be stillborn. Balancing between "Things that Kill you" and progress on your strategy requires careful, constant management of resources. You can free up internal resources by removing priority from the "Things that make you Happy," and redirecting them to the most critical initiatives. Next, take a serious look at those "Things that Eat You" to ensure they are receiving the right amount of attention and won't end up sneaking up on you.

Fully resourcing the "Things that Kill you" without over staffing them, ensuring the "Things that Eat you" are resourced appropriately based on their severity, and moving the "Things that make You Happy" off of the list will provide the best support possible to your change initiative. If that still isn't sufficient, utilize outside resources anywhere that their help can support those initiatives with the highest "system effect" or return on investment.

In addition to developing a focus on the right priorities, once you establish a game plan, it cannot be abandoned at the first sign of trouble. While adjustments are fine, too much "global" reprioritization of your initiatives can induce organizational schizophrenia. If you want your associates to support and follow you in achieving the business goals, make sure your own support for the plan remains stable and your course corrections are clearly justified.

Thus far, you will have expended tremendous effort to get the change initiative off the ground, and your engagement factor should begin to swell. Keeping the entire team focused on objective achievement, while performing complementary team-based activities and responding when things begin to fall behind, is made easier by deploying a set of "Pull Behavior" tools.

"Pull Behaviors" will help to change your culture from within by using a standardized set of "triggers" to request a response-based action (think of stopping at a stoplight) to correct an abnormality. The three components of the system include the trigger or "request" for action, people who understand it's their responsibility and are trained to "provide" a response to the trigger, and a "Standardized Work" set of defined responses that serve to "guide" the solution.

Pull behaviors create a community effort around the correction of performance abnormalities and it's this timely response that minimizes their damage, helping to drive the motives for "blame" out of the culture.

Lean into your change initiative

The most powerful tool set you will find to implement and reap benefits from your change initiative comes in the form of Lean Enterprise. Regardless of the type of business—manufacturing, services, health care, etc.—Lean has proven techniques to help understand your customer's needs and provide value added activities exactly at the rate they are required. Although Lean utilizes a series of older tools, it offers two critical differences that make it far more effective. First, it recognizes that broad engagement is required for success. Second, it utilizes tools that are inter-dependent; in other words, using them individually won't give you the impact you want. In the simplest of terms, Lean demands that you intimately understand your customers and market, and utilize its rate of demand or *takt*, to build systems that are flexible enough to cost-effectively respond to that demand and its changes. The Lean tools will enable you to "flow" activities at *takt,* while pull behaviors will mobilize your team to provide rapid response to changes. A well-implemented Lean tool set can yield truly amazing results.

Monitor your progress!

A new change initiative deserves a refreshed set of business metrics to go with it. While that doesn't require you to change or eliminate all of the traditional metrics, the application of clear benchmarks and objectives will provide renewed focus. It's easy to overburden an organization by measuring everything under the sun, so keep your key metrics list simple and focused on business-critical measurements. Maintain timely review cycles that are in line with your ability to take action on what you learn from them. As quickly as you can, try to evolve them away from looking solely at results and toward predictive measures that are more helpful in steering the business. The right set of metrics, combined with timely review and follow up, will serve to energize organizational engagement.

Each of the improvements that are reaped from your change initiative will require stability and support to be sustained. Although we've spent a considerable amount of time offering engagement approaches for the activities around your change strategy, the thrust of this book has been toward driving change and achieving goals. Most likely, all of us have worked in companies that were great at achieving an objective, but which weren't as good at sustaining the gains. Improvements will fall apart if we fail to understand the "maintenance manual" for the changes. A well-designed process audit program is a useful tool to help guide the construction of that "manual" while at the same time using the increase in associate involvement to broaden engagement. Your system design activity should include participation from *all* members of the organization, and positioning the auditing topic/activities as far forward of the results as possible can yield the most positive impact.

Make Improvement Systemic!

The final element of sustainability is to develop a systemic approach in which all of the improvements can find their way into your business processes. Doing this will require identifying and separating your "core processes" from the larger group of all of your business processes. These core process lists will very likely follow common themes within different types of businesses but should include, at minimum, processes that cover customer-facing activities, development of offerings, delivery of offerings, associate development, management of information, and Leadership. A critical success factor in building sustainability is to assign a champion or owner to each core process and their critical sub-processes. They will assume responsibility for leading a team in monitoring results (metrics) and using them to actively evolve the processes effectiveness. This is the step that constitutes the "cement" of sustainability for your improvements.

That should summarize it all. While there is plenty of supporting detail to help you in each of the chapters, every unique business situation will serve as an individual test to many of these approaches. This is where numerous Lean implementations have served me well, teaching me that while the details of the implementation will always change, they will equally be resolved by the details of the solutions. A simplified "high level" approach is what should remain consistent in order to achieve the desired result.

Good luck sustaining your gains!

Addendum

"I'm not on board with the changes you're advocating and am instructing you to stop with them. Further, there will be no discussion of this with anyone at corporate headquarters. This plant is doing just fine without their help."

My boss, the plant manager was explicit, and any attempts to strengthen my point only frustrated him more, causing him to terminate the discussion abruptly.

"Here is a copy of your self-appraisal. I'd like you to fill it out with your own impression of your performance and return it to me by the end of the week."

I'd only been on his staff for just a few months and, unbeknownst to me, had more or less been imposed upon him by a senior executive who wanted to stimulate some change from underneath—career avoidance advice for any newcomers to management. Our honeymoon hadn't been stellar, and we seemed to be at odds at every turn. He had built an accomplished profit machine, winning credit year after year for financial performance that always exceeded his business plans. Such consistent performance was the result of a number of different things, but a key element was his very firm control of everything within the facility's four walls and a nearly military style of execution—borne of his own past. Any level of change was scrutinized heavily for its downside, and even the slightest chance of a negative impact would stop it until it could be reworked to be risk-free. The rate of change was agonizingly slow, and because consistency of results was what he had been so well-rewarded for, he was understandably careful to protect it.

When I completed my self-appraisal a few days later and attempted to return it as instructed, he asked me to hang on to it, and through the course of a couple of reminders over the next couple of weeks, continued to put it off, opting not to discuss it. I turned it in, unchanged, at year end when my regular annual appraisal was due, and he returned it virtually unchanged and with a very high rating, something I found confusing.

Over time, he gained sufficient confidence in me to begin allowing limited experimentation with some of the improvements I'd been proposing. Still, because of his requirement to modify them until they were entirely risk-free, our improvement progress still wasn't great. The following year, a significant event occurred that completely altered the market dynamic. Our largest customer (and the market leader) entered into a supply agreement with our primary competitor, who had just been purchased by one of their larger suppliers. The agreement switched sourcing of many of the products we'd been providing that customer to our competitor, impacting more than 20% of our total business revenue. In a single move, they literally inverted our respective market positions overnight, triggered by that most powerful of market forces—price. Not only did we lose a huge segment of our market share, but we were also forced simultaneously to reduce our pricing on the balance of the products we sold to that customer.

The event was an apocalypse from the perspective of our business. Pressure to stabilize profitability in the face of such a radical market shift built instantly, and it opened the doors for a much more rapid rate of change than anyone could have imagined. Although it had taken this general manager 22 years to perfect his profit machine, it took only a few months and a sudden shift in the market to unravel it. In the end, he was left with no choice but to risk more radical improvement attempts in response to the market changes, driving a level of risk that he truly struggled with. Feeling frustrated, he retired in its midst.

The profit engine had fallen off the tracks, and suddenly there was a receptiveness to change borne of the urgency to survive. Among it all, a key element of the business model he had built—its stellar responsiveness and almost mechanical execution—remained well-preserved, and it was instrumental in helping us to capitalize on opportunities to regain sales volume every time our competitor encountered performance problems, which happened frequently.

A key lesson for me was that consistency of performance is a huge asset to any business, and it originates with managerial discipline. The predictability of performance that it breeds—consistency of expectations, regular achievement of metric targets, and careful evolution of operational processes—can also have the side-effect of stifling improvement if you aren't careful. That general manager's fear wasn't rooted in the threat of change, but that changes of excessive magnitude or speed might compromise results. He had long ago come to understand a lesson that he would end up teaching me: You can only change as fast as the organization can follow, and you don't want to induce change at a rate that destroys all of the embedded disciplines in the organization. Later on, I added a counter-balanced learning that the level of effort you expend in preparing people for change will return itself in an accelerated rate of adoption. He advocated using proven techniques in a highly-controlled environment in a way that would move results forward without any chance of adverse effects. Although his management style delivered great results, his own understanding of the behavioral impact was mostly one-sided and resulted in good performance that was sub-optimized.

Ultimately, we were able to re-stabilize profitability in the business, albeit at a lower overall level. The market made a permanent adjustment, commoditizing the product and forever sacrificing its pricing premium. Our return to consistency was attributable in part to a strong commitment to Lean Enterprise and also the same attribute that had gotten them there in the first place: world-class customer responsiveness and an organization-wide commitment to deliver consistently excellent performance. It was a basic expectation within that business's culture that couldn't be derailed even by a major market event.

Hopefully, my commitment to provide concise and simple concepts for leading business transformation has been delivered upon. My friend's belief that business leaders are highly intelligent people whose tendency to over-complicate problems seems accurate enough. But I often find their approaches or solutions for many business issues too often exclude sufficient consideration for the human dynamic, leading to confusion and failure. An essential lesson of leadership lies in understanding that complexity makes it harder for associates to follow any approach, thereby reducing speed, impairing results, and potentially stalling improvement.

Addressing complex problems with simple solutions takes remarkable discipline. The fact is, the more effort you expend on simplification, the less effort will be required for the actual activities and contingencies. The better you get at it, the greater speed your initiatives will gain, benefiting from their superior ease of associate understanding and engagement.

This book is an accumulation of real experiences and is about 80% based in fact. Don't think for a minute that I've discounted or ignored the complexity that exists in many of the situations covered in this book. Having actually lived them, every scenario offered as an example carried its own "how-to" lesson in simplification. The trick is to strip the problem to its basic needs and focus the team on providing great solutions as they go along.

Keeping the organization working on problems at their correct levels avoids the complexity that comes from trying to work on too many diverse root causes, maintaining their span of control. That's the essence of simplification—not to ignore the complexity, but simply to isolate it at the most appropriate place for people to work on it and not allow it to accumulate into something too large to control.

All of the concepts I've introduced—cycles of response, reconnoitering, triangulation and others—are intended to focus your attention on identification of the contributors to your problems, leading to positive actions that will resolve them. They serve as reality checkpoints at times when massive amounts of information might confuse and create disarray.

Change initiatives attract complexity, but don't allow it to stop you or intimidate you from getting started. The choices often made in order to preserve a current state of performance, while averting risk or performance loss, can frequently be detrimental to the long-term health of a business. Let's close with one final Machiavelli quote:

"The wise man does at once what the fool does finally!"

So, now that you've finished the book, stop contemplating your change initiative, go paint some bullseyes on your objectives and let some air out of your tires to get rolling!

Lowell Puls

Takt-ical Terminology
A Glossary of unique Terms

Consistentize – The use of formalized disciplines to stabilize the performance of key business processes across a business. In this book it refers to the six critical business processes of Leadership, Strategy, Customer RIF, Human Resources ADAPT, Process Improvement Management (PIM), and Results Management.

Directional – Used as in directional estimates, directional assessments, or directional effects. This term indicates a general level of data accuracy that merely needs to be sufficient enough to tell the decision maker which of a limited number of strategic choices makes the most sense.

Jumping to Contusions – Occurs when a conclusion is drawn based on incomplete or partial evidence. This often results in rework effort and lost opportunities, hence the reference to painful contusions.

Pareto – Taken from the Pareto Principle (also called the 80/20 rule) and the pareto chart (Bar and line chart combination). In this book, pareto level suggests the elemental components that contribute to a summary metric or, the list of causes the support or create a result.

Pull Behaviors – Are the desired responses to process or performance abnormalities. They are called "Pull" because of their linkage to some type of trigger (audible or visual) that requests (pulls) intervention by an associate who is assigned responsibility for that process.

Response-Ability – Used with the titles of leadership, or management; response-ability indicates the need for a leader/manager to be personally responsive to the needs of the organization at her/his fullest capability, as well as to expect a similar level of response from all associates.

Takt – a German word describing the baton used by an orchestra direct to establish the rhythm of an orchestra. In Lean Enterprise, Takt refers to the rhythm or pace of the marketplace, as in units, service opportunities, patients, or calls received in a given time period.

Takt Time – This is the conversion of **demand into the time available to fulfill that demand.** The formula for takt time is Demand / Time available. In this formula, time available can be more complicated as it is impacted by assets available, operating hours, staffing levels, etc.

Thruput – The term Thruput is a metric that is meant to represent the aggregate time that it takes to manufacture a product or deliver a service from it's beginning to its end form. Generally, thruput is measured for a single facility, example; Manufacturing a product from raw material to finished product place in a box for shipment. Thruput differs from both cycle time and takt time in that it is accumulative through several processes.

Key Process Flow Diagrams

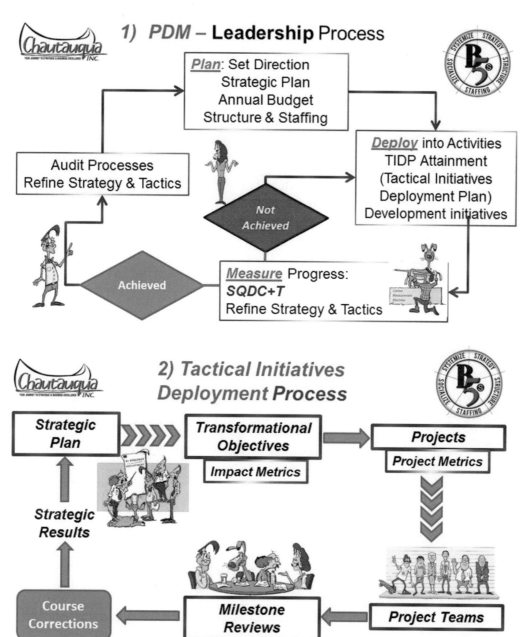

1) *PDM* – **Leadership** Process

Plan: Set Direction
Strategic Plan
Annual Budget
Structure & Staffing

Audit Processes
Refine Strategy & Tactics

Deploy into Activities
TIDP Attainment
(Tactical Initiatives
Deployment Plan)
Development initiatives

Not Achieved

Achieved

Measure Progress:
SQDC+T
Refine Strategy & Tactics

2) *Tactical Initiatives Deployment Process*

Strategic Plan

Transformational Objectives
Impact Metrics

Projects
Project Metrics

Strategic Results

Course Corrections

Milestone Reviews

Project Teams

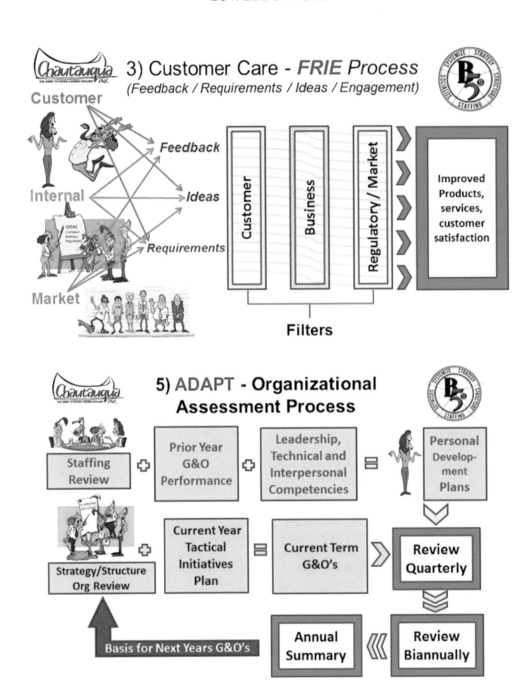

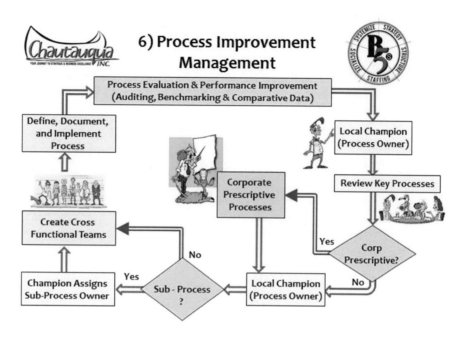

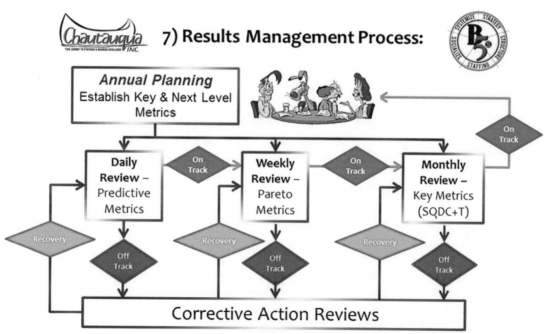

Lean Enterprise Templates

LEAP LEAN Excellence Assessment Process	Tool Priorities / Road Map				
	Novice (just beginning)	Experimenters (early stages)	Believers (turning the corner)	Skilled Implementers	Masters of ovement
	1 Points	2 Points	3 Points	4 Points	5 Points
Flow Tools (Value Stream Maps, Continuous Flow, Pull Systems)	**1** (all tools)	**1** (all tools)	**1** (Flow/Pull)	**3** (Flow)	**4** (VSM - New Map)
Standard Work (5s, Standard Work, Total Productive Maintenance, Setup Reduction)	**2** (5s)	**4** (5s / Std Work)	**3** (5s / Std Work)	**1** (Std. Work)	**1** (Std. Work)
Jidoka Tools (Error Proofing and Problem Resolution, Visual Systems, Autonomation)	**3** (Visuals)	**2** (Visuals)	**2** (Visuals)	**2** (E/P and Visuals)	**2** (E/P and Visuals)
Continuous Improvement (Training and Engagement, Measurement Systems)	**4** (Metrics)	**3** (Training)	**4** (Training)	**4** (Training)	**3** (Training)
Savings Potential	30%+++	30%+	20-30%	15-20%	5-15%

LEAP	Lean Excellence Assessment Process: Tool Priorities / Road Map				Chautauqua INC.
	Novice (shoppers)	**Experimenters** (toes in the water)	**Believers** (turning the corner)	**Skilled Implementers**	**Improvement Masters**
	1 Points	2 Points	3 Points	4 Points	5 Points
Condition of the Environment	Use of visuals is not evident, cleanliness isn't supported by a process, materials not in flow aren't clearly controlled	Visual indicators are used by management to resolve abnormalities. Materials not in flow are better controlled. Overall cleanliness is good in pockets.	Sort, Straighten, Shine are in place. Visuals for production pace and abnormality response are used by management. Scrap/Rework is minimal and controlled	The environment is visual to all associates with indicators for most abnormalities in place. Cleanliness, materials, and contamination are well controlled.	The environment is visual to outsiders. Cleanliness is high and contamination absent. Abnormalities are clearly identified, and correctvie response is rapid.
Lean Tools in Use	Tool usage is pocketed and isolated. Some evidence of sort or straighten, minimal visuals, pacemaker is known but not managed	Tool usage (5s, pull systems) is still limited to pacemaker or critical work centers. Takt and hruput time in the value stream is known.	Value stream maps extend to the cell level, pacemaker is the schedule point and kanban is in use. 5s, Flow, and Standard work are taking shape.	Most Lean tools are in use, with flow, pull, and 5s highly evolved. Standard work is progressing and TPM and Six Sigma are in early stages.	All lean tools show advanced levels of implementation. TPM and Six Sigma projects are scheduled. Workforce flexibility is high and tied closely to takt levels.
Cultural Indicators	Management and associates lead separate lives: decision making is at higher levels, autonomy isn't promoted. Minimal evidence of training or continuous improvement activities.	Visuals response remains management driven. Some business metrics and minimal cell metrics are posted. Team leaders have limited leadership roles.	Management leads/teaches corrective actions with team participation. Team leaders have many day to day leadership responsibilities.	Management personnel audit process conformance while team leaders have evolved into tool champions. Participation in Continuous Improvement efforts is high	Improvement efforts are led by team leaders with high levels of team participation. "Point lesson" oontinuous improvement events are ongoing and associate led.
Performance Results	Profitable (maybe) but input losses (labor material, capacity) are indicated by presence of visible scrap, productivity and downtime issues. Day to day performance is unstable.	Isolated improvements in flow and quality are evident. Some cell level metrics are posted and goals attained. Overall objective attainment is suboptimal and day to day performance is sporadic.	Improvements are evident through consistent Takt and labor objective attainment. Management is auditing and day to day performance is stable.	All metrics show improvement with cell targets, OEE and performance at the pacemaker and critical work centers consistently setting new highs. Financial performance is also achieving new levels.	All metrics are achieving optimum levels. All auditing is supported by an action/ feedback loop to support continuous improvement. Business profitability is constantly optimized.
Savings Potential	30%+++	30%+	20-30%	15-20%	5-15%

Lean Tool Usage Assessment - Part 1

Level	Flow Tools			Standard Work Tools			
	VSM	Continuous Flow	Pull Systems	5 s	Standard Work	TPM	Set Up Reduction
Novice	No Map exists Facility thruput is known	Flow is minimal. Few connections are visible	Some kanbans exist, but with unclear triggering / WIP limits	Isolated cleanup is not supported by a process	Basic process instructions exist	Some Preventive Maintenance exists	Some set-up processes are documented
Experimenters	A current state map exists	Schedule point may be defined, Takt is known, some processes are connected	Kanbans exist ahead of the schedule point	1S and 2S are completed in some areas	Some Standard Work exists	PM is deployed and performed	SMED priorities have been ID'd in the value stream with metrics
Believers	Current and Future state maps exist	The schedule point and finished goods strategy are defined, Some cells are linked and takt is deployed	Kanban deployed internally upstream from the schedule point	3S is implemented facility-wide	Standard Work is takt based and partially deployed	TPM priorities are in place and plans in process	Critical Work Centers have completed SMED
Skilled Implementers	A future state map has been completed for the facility	Work pulls to the schedule point and flows from it. Resources flex with changes in takt	Kanban / Supermarkets deployed internally and to critical suppliers	4S is Standardized facilitywide	Standard Work includes Safety and TPM - is developed by Operators	Autonomous Maintenance is deployed	All setups have completed SMED, are documented and standardized
Improvement Masters	Multiple Generations of current/future state maps are completed	Minimal increments of flow have been achieved. Kanban use has been minimized. All resources flex with changes in takt.	All materials movement internal and external is pull based. Kanbans have been minimized.	5S is Sustained: All associates participate	Std Work is deployed plantwide and operator maintained	Autonomous Maintenance/ Six Sigma are Sustained	Sustained cycles of improvement have enabled best in class metrics

Lean Tool Usage Assessment - Part 2

Level	Jidoka Tools			Continuous Improvement Tools		
	Error Proofing	Visual Systems	Autonomation	Six Sigma	Training	Metrics
Novice	Defect containment is in place	Minimal visuals are in place for facility safety and machine uptime	Minimal separation of man/machine activities in place	Minimal/Limited statistical process controls are in use	On-the-job training is conducted and documented	Minimal measurements are in place
Experimenters	Detection is iin place for known defects	Management visuals for pacing and production status, cell safety control points, exist	Opportunities for associates to run multiple machines are ID'd or implemented	Some process charting is in place. Green Belts are being developed	Key managers are being developed into trainers and auditors	Management monitors / maintains limited cell and business level metrics
Believers	Prevention for known defects is deployed	Mgmt and Group Leads respond to visuals for safety, 5s, production status, and issues	Self stop features have been added to enable operators to run multiple machines	Green Belts are in place, a black belt resource is available, workcells have quality process champions	Select associates are developing as tool champions and green/yellow belts	Mgmt uses business metrics to set priorities, and plan improvements. Cell level metrics are associate monitored
Skilled Implementers	Most known defects have been eliminated	Associates respond to visual triggers for Safety, Production Status,and abnormalities	All machines have self-stop and andons to enable operators load/unload	Green and Yellow Belt resources are responsible for process quality. A black belt resource is available.	Managers and key associates are teachers and lead training and problem solving	Well deployed cell and business metrics engage associates in identifying improvement needs
Improvement Masters	Systematic prevention of potential defects is in place	Visuals deployment is so thorough that visitors understand abnormalities. Linked visuals convey all status needs.	Self stop and auto unload enable operators to use one-button start only for machines	A resident black belt assigns project priorities. Green belt (professional) and Yellow Belt (Associate) resources are available	Associate training enables them tlo lead response efforts, root cause analysis and Improvements	Measurement focus has evolved from results to predictive metrics. Associates engage to preempt negative trends.

Lean Tool Interrelationships

Lean Tool Interrelationships

LEAP — LEAN Excellence Assessment Process

Lean Tools Linkage	VSM	Continuous Flow	Pull	5s	Standard Work	TPM	Set up Reduction	Error Proofing	Visual Management	Autonomation
VSM	Defines Improvement Priorities	VS Interruptions	System View - Multiple Loops	5s visuals run the system	VSM Takt is the time basis for SW	Critical WC's are ID'd in VSM	SR reduced total thruput time	EP provides yield improvement	The status /actions of the V/S are visual	Autonomation improves V/S efficiency & effectiveness
Continuous Flow		Predictable Thruput	Takt based Pull / flow quantities	Clutter inhibits Flow	Takt is the time basis for SW	TPM Yield improves flow	SR improves flow w/reduced batch & cue	E/P Yield Improvements accelerate flow	Good flow can be experienced visually	Flow sustainment is facilitated
Pull			Demand Management	Visual triggers govern Pull activities	Pull Triggers incorporated into SW	Stan Wk Includes Pull elements	Reduced Batch/Lots/ Kanbans	Pull Requires maximized EP yield	Production controls move to a visual basis	Autonomation improves the predictability of pull response
5s				Workplace Organization and Safety	5s is included in Standard Work	TPM requires 5s elements	SU Tools are organized in 5s	Error Proofing controls ID'd	5s improves the effectiveness of visual controls	Operator activity can support 5s
Standard Work					Standardizes Workplace Activity	Autonomous Maintenance is in Std. Work	Stan Wk Includes SR elements	Stan Wk includes EP elements	Visual elements support SW tasks and tools	Autonomation is supported by the Standard Work
TPM						Maximizes Equipment Performance	Reduced Setups tied to Machine improvements	E/P built in through machine improvements	Machine status factors are made visual	TPM supports and improves autonomation
Set up Reduction							Reduces non value add content	Setup improvements include EP	Tools and Std Work for setups are visual	Set-up reduction improvements enable autonomation
Error Proofing								Improves Process Yield	Poke Yokes have visual indentification	E/P improvements facilitate autonomation
Visual Management									Focuses behaviors and builds sustainment	Visual indicators support Autonomation
Autonomation										Operators focus moves to value-add, from mundane work